MICHAEL'S GEMSTONE DICTIONARY

Metaphysical properties of gems and minerals
according to the Michael Teaching.

Channeled by
JP Van Hulle

Written by
Judithann H. David Ph.D.

Third Edition: April, 1987

MICHAEL'S
GEMSTONE DICTIONARY

Metaphysical properties of gems and minerals
according to the Michael Teaching

Published by the Michael Educational Foundation and Touchstone in
Orinda, California

For information write:
Michael Educational Foundation
10 Muth Drive
Orinda, California 94563
USA

Third Edition, April, 1987

This book is dedicated to my beloved husband, Desai,
my precious daughter, Juliana, and to my mother
who worked to make this bookpossible even
though she doesn't "believe" in Michael.
Judie

I dedicate this work to my darlings: Aaron, Penny,
and Jessica and with love and gratitude to my
ever loyal parents: Joy and John Perasso.
Thank you.
JP

TABLE OF CONTENTS

    Server: Service to others
    Priest: Inspiration
    Artisan: Creativity
    Sage: Wisdom
    Warrior: Productivity
    King: Mastery
    Scholar: Knowledge

    Growth
    Re-evaluation
    Acceptance
    Discrimination
    Dominance
    Submission
    Stagnation

    Repression
    Passion
    Caution
    Power
    Perserverance
    Aggression
    Observation

    Stoic
    Spiritualist
    Skeptic
    Idealist
    Cynic
    Realist
    Pragmatist

PREFACE

Since that evening in November of 1984, when a group of us received channeling from Michael on the 35 or so gemstones that relate to the roles and overleaves, we have gotten more and more interested in gemstones and how they affect the physical body. For the last year or so, Michael students have been seen with their list of stones haunting gem shows and lapidaries. With the exception of the original group of gemstones we received information about, all the gemstones and minerals listed are included because some Michael student was attracted to it, and brought it in for channeling. Subsequently, we have looked them up in gemological texts trying to ascertain if the name we were given at a gem show is accurate. While there may be some inaccuracies or misidentifaction of minerals, I think we have kept it at a minimum. Our hope is you will take the information we have collected here and have as much fun selecting gemstones and minerals for you own use as we have.

So. who is Michael and what is the Michael Teaching? We would like to quote Clark (4) who answers this question very succinctly in "The Michael Connection" a newsletter.

The main goal of the Michael Teaching is agape or unconditional love.

The Michael Teaching views life as a learning game in which fragments of the Tao--that essential part of each human being--sets up lessons which continue over lifetimes. These lessons are learned via the personality which Essence chooses each lifetime. Michael teaches us what the components of the personality are so that we can learn to use and see these components in ourselves and in others. In that way we can learn to understand why human beings behave as they do--the perfection of life as it is.

Michael is composed of 1050 individual Essences who have lived on the physical plane and now teach from another plane.

1

Many Essences on the physical plane have agreed to learn from Michael, although it is often on a personality level that we reap the benefits of this Teaching. Michael usually speaks through human "channels" who have agreed (on an Essence level) to assist Michael with their Teaching.

The entity, Michael, teaches as part of their progression through the circle of existence. This circle leads from the Tao, through the physical plane and 6 other planes of existence, and back to the Tao again. Thus we can say that no person, essence or entity is "ahead" or "behind" another, but only that they occupy a different place on the circle.

The mission of the Michael entity in their Teaching is to help prepare the planet in its current shift from a "me first" attitude to one of more of an identification between human beings, in which people learn to see others as they see themselves, therefore deserving of the same love and respect.

One of the most basic and important principles of the Michael Teaching is that is is not a religion or a belief system. Michael encourages their students to "self-validate" all of the information they receive. Some of the most important and challenging lessons that Michael students receive revolve around the issue of self-validation.

Being a Michael student involves no uniformity of belief, no required term of study and often very little else beyond a willingness to learn and to use those lessons which seem appropriate in your life.

A Message from MICHAEL. . .

We have presented all of the information we teach so people can have their lives work in a more integrated and balanced fashion as they go through the lessons they are learning on the physical plane. Being physical means you are to *use* the physical and find out how to be competent areound physical things as well. It also means you are to be in complete acceptance of all things physical.

Many religious and philosophical organizations encourage you to rise above the physical as you get to be an older soul. We say you cannot rise above the place where you are. As long as you have a physical body, it is important to use the physical body appropriately and gently or you will not be able to have higher centered experiences or evolve eventually to a higher than physical state.

Because of this fact, we find it extremely important that people use the various tools available to them on the physical plane to be in balance, and to be healed: that they use their body appropriately and in a sacred fashion: that they take care of themselves physically while they pay attention in other ways to their emotional, psychological and spiritual natures.

Gemstones and minerals are one of the tools available on the physical plane and are something that everyone uses whether they realize it or not. Almost no one is unaffected by stones. You see a pretty rock--you pick it up. You put it in your pocket. You don't even know why you like it. If you have the conscious knowledge of what is behind the usefulness of a particular stone, what happens is that the use will be much more powerful. With conscious knowledge, you increase onehundredfold the power of the rock in your life that you were using anyway by having it close to you.

The benefit of using an appropriate stone is that it makes life easier. It makes you more capable of being balanced, of having good communication with others, and of getting along

3

well with others. Even when you are all alone, you can use the appropriate gemstone for any of your intellectual, physical, emotional or spiritual types of work. So, since you have the benefit of these gifts while you are on the physical plane, we would like you to use them to their fullest extent. Our work gets done here on the physical plane when people get to experience agape; people get to experience truth; and people get to experience their physicality at its highest level.

GEMSTONES
The Energies of Gemstones and How to Use Them

You are about to start a very interesting journey: that of understanding how the energy of gemstones and minerals affect our body and psychological functioning. Stones, like other things of this planet, embody a certain kind of energy and each stone has a specific purpose or value that can be used by human beings. By attuning yourself to the information about gemstones that we are presenting here, you can use stones and gems to channel these different types of energy for healing, and balancing and in order to accentuate the qualities to which they correspond.

This works because all gemstones and minerals have a crystalline structure that pick up electro-magnetic currents which then flow through your body at a particular frequency which creates an electrochemical response in the body. There is research to indicate that healing can be speeded up by running electrical impulses through the body at a particular frequency.

The knowledge made available in this material relates to the higher kinesthetic center which deals with manipulating energy and appreciating beauty. Energy in its most solid form manifests as physical objects and each object resonates at its particular energetic level. Of the solid inanimate objects in the earth, gems and gemstones are the most concentrated form of energy. Almost all stones are mostly male energied (or focused energy) being concentrated and crystalline. A stone in its natural state (rough, uncut, unpolished) is more female energied (unfocused energy) than a stone that has been cut and faceted. The more perfect the stone and symmetrical the faceting, the more male energied it is.

For the purpose of receiving energy from stones, what matters is their chemical composition, but not their degree of perfection, whether they be in a natural state, man-made, cut, polished or of gem quality. With a man-made stone, it is

5

important to find out the chemical compositon, as this affects its nature. For example, a Cubic Zirconia is a man-made Garnet even though it is presented as a substitute for Diamonds, and corresponds to productivity (a warrior quality) rather than mastery (a king quality).

The size of a stone does not particularly matter as a very small stone can produce enough energy to stimulate your body. A stone which is placed within a foot or so of your body will affect it within minutes. If a stone is placed in a room, the energy of the stone will permeate the room in about three weeks and take another week to dissipate if removed.

When a stone has more than one type of rock running through it, one will receive the effects of both. There are a few stones that are affected by the degree of clarity. One, of course, is rock crystal. Because this stone is for "observation" and assists one in "seeing" clearly, the more perfectly clear the crystal, the more clarity it produces. Another stone that is affected by the degree of clarity is Chrysocolla.

On an essence level, we do differentiate between cut and uncut stones, flawed or perfect, because our essence responds energetically to the beauty of a stone. Remember that the positive pole of the higher kinesthetic center is beauty, and beauty is a manifestation of energy in a particularly refined state. The body, however, does not differentiate on this level and flaws do not affect the energy of the stone. In order to use the information presented here, we are dealing with the energy response on a bodily level. Thus, you can buy the less expensive flawed stones and receive maximum benefit.

When selecting gemstones for your own use, the most important guideline is that you find the stone attractive. That is your body's way of telling you that it's the right one for you. The gemstone will have a specific effect on you whether you are aware of what it does or not. However, it seems the conscious knowledge of the gemstone's properties combined with the use of that gemstone is synergistic and the effect of gemstones worn with awareness is more powerful.

We have received channeling on over 300 different minerals

and gemstones. This can be a bit confusing to the novice who might wonder where to start and which stones are the most important. Of course, any stone that is attractive to you is important, but we can give you a few guidelines. In the section on roles and overleaves you will find listed almost all the most commonly available and popular stones. There is a chart for each section and for each role, goal, etc., there is one stone set in capital letters. This is the stone we were originally given as most reflecting the qualities of the role or overleaf with which it is associated. Note that many of the precious stones are associated with the roles such as Diamonds, Rubies and Sapphires. Note that most of the Jades are associated with the attitudes. Pay particular attention to the stones listed in the centers which includes Lapis Lazuli, Pearls and Amber. And everyone should have something for the instinctive center (to calm survival fears) which includes Bone, Ivory or Shell.

Of equal importance is keeping the chakras unblocked, aligned and balanced. The Aventurines (Red, blue and green) are very useful for this as well as some others. Next, check out the stones in the section on balance. Michael emphasizes strongly the necessity for balance. Malachite is probably the most powerful and generally useful stone in this regard. Three other stones are a must: Rose Quartz to be in touch with your essence, Flourite to clear the aura, and Grey Jade for reducing tension. After playing with this group of probably 45 or 50 stones. You can then branch out into some of the other areas into lesser known gemstones and minerals. They are usually available at gem shows and are great fun to hunt down as well as quite inexpensive.

After being worn for a while, a gemstone or mineral can be drained of its energy, or soak up undesirable energies occurring in its proximity. There are a number of ways to restore a gemstone or mineral to its original freshness; i.e., clean it up. 1) Place it in rock salt for 3 to 30 days. The problem with this method is that some minerals or gemstones are harmed by the salt such as Pearls or Halite. 2) Place it in the freezer for three hours to three days. 3) Selenite can be used to clean and recharge minerals and gemstones. Place the gemstone or mineral on top of the round, mushroomy type of Selenite. With Selenite that occurs in long crystals; first place the Selenite to point at a rock crystal and set the rock crystal to point at the gemstone or mineral you want to affect.

7

ROLES and OVERLEAVES

The gemstones and minerals listed in this section are categorized according to Michael's view of the universe. The use of these stones is a concrete way to learn and experience various aspects of the Michael teaching. For those who are not that familiar with the Michael teaching or who are new students, an effort has been made to define relevant terms and concepts clearly. You can also think of the gemstones and minerals as reflecting various qualities and look at each in terms of the quality you want to pull into your life or "space." For example, warrior stones all reflect the quality of productivity and organized efficiency while those stones listed under the category of priest, all reflect a quality of inspiration and ability to see the larger picture.

With regard to stones that are especially specific to a particular role, one can be of any role and use any other role's stones effectively with certain qualifications. An example is Psilomelane which is described as enabling a king to be powerful and influential, etc. While a king would find this rock useful in any area they wished to be powerful, other roles would find the rock useful only in mastery or skills that are kinglike. A scholar, for example, would not experience a more powerful thirst for knowledge, but would be more powerful in the mastery of skills necessary to acquire knowledge. When in doubt, remember the general rule of thumb that if you are attracted to a rock or gemstone, it will be of value to you.

This section is composed of six parts: Roles, Goals, Modes, Attitudes, Centers and Chief Features. The latter five are known as the overleaves. The role describes one's essence or the way of "being" one has throughout one's lives. The overleaves describe the basic personality characteristics and change with each lifetime to provide a variety of different lessons. Brief definitions are given of each term in the material that follows. A chart showing the basic organization of a section is included as the last page of each section.

For each role, goal, etc., there is a positive and negative pole; i.e., a positive and negative way of manifesting that energy. The gemstones reflect only positive energy and will pull you into the positive pole of the role, goal, etc. It is useful to select stones that are associated with your own role and overleaves to give yourself a chance to experience functioning in the positive poles on a consistent basis. It is also interesting and useful to select stones associated with other roles and overleaves to pull different ways of being into your life. For example, if you need to go into a difficult situation with your eyes open, you might wish to choose Jet, a stone for cynicism even though you are not a cynic. Or if you are a cynic, and a little weary of it, you might select some Lavendar Jade to pull a little optimism into your life.

ROLES

ROLE: Essence's role is it's primary way of being or the "underlying perception through which it chooses to experience its lessons in a cycle of lifetimes."(1)

SERVER: Servers "inspire and care for others by serving them." (I) They are nurturant, care-taking, loving, inspiring, other-directed, practical, trustworthy, and friendly.
CLINOCHLORE: Helps all roles to get in touch with their server qualities.
CLINOZOISITE: (Brown, Lt. green or gray green in color). Makes servers better able to serve themselves. Servers in their focus on service often tend to forget that they need to take care of and serve themselves as well to remain balanced.
CUPROLITE: For service, practicality, and attention to detail. Enables servers to work in a very practical, grounded way with the ability to pay attention to the details of what needs to be done.
RED TO BROWN FELDSPAR: Balances, grounds, and integrates mature and old servers.
HELIODOR: Balances old and mature servers. More powerful than rubies, but harder to find. Can feel very mellow about serving and approach giving to others in a relaxed fashion without feeling that one is being victimized or trapped in any

way or allowing that to happen. One of the most comforting types of stones to wear.

RUBY: Makes one feel giving and happy about being able to be of service to others. Reduces resentment about same.

WHITE SAPPHIRE: Keeps one serving oneself appropriately by making sure one does nice things for oneself. Enables one to be gentle with oneself and helps prevent needless suffering. Useful for all roles, but especially servers.

PURPLE SPINEL: Most useful when one is being victimized around serving or feels that one is; enables one to pull out of being a victim and gain control. A server stone since this most often happens to servers. Also, aids communication with those at least 20 years older or younger than yourself. A generation gap stone.

SYLVITE: Enables a Server to be powerful in whatever area they choose. Particularly empowers Servers in manifesting the positive pole of their role.

PINK ZOISITE: (Also called Thulite). Balances infant, baby and young servers.

GREEN ZOISITE: (with Ruby Crystals--ANYOLITE) General purpose for servers in positions of great power or who wish to manifest powerfully. Useful for other roles when in a position of service to others: can use one's power very effectively to heal or influence others when it is in their best interests.

PRIEST: **Priests are concerned with the spiritual welfare of others. They are inspirational, compassionate, emotionally connected, healing and warm.**

AXINITE: For infant, baby and young priests. Keeps them from going overboard into total zealousness, unable to maintain balance and being totally fanatical about things. Older soul ages rarely allow themselves to go overboard this much.

ALBITE FELDSPAR: (Blue, clear & white). Balances, grounds and integrates mature and old priests.

LIGHT BLUE SAPPHIRE: Inspirational. Produces inspired conceptual thoughts. Wear when you want to feel excited about life; that it will really work. Good for therapists as it will inspire them to see through people's blocks and ways to work them out. With regard to the color variation of blue sapphires from light to dark blue: blue Sapphires in general

10

relate to the fluid roles. The darker the blue, the more creative it is and the lighter the blue, the more intellectually centered and philosophical it is.

SPHENE: (Also called Titanite). Balancing for priests. Makes them feel they can be really compassionate. Particularly useful for priests and other roles in situations that put a strain on one's compassion such as working in a hospital or with very disturbed or crazy people for extended periods of time. Each color is for a different soul perception.

  BLACK & BROWN: Infant priests
  CLEAR: Baby priests
  YELLOW & GREEN: Mature priests
  ROSE-RED: Old priests

VANADANITE: For inspiration. Often occurs with quartz crystal so combines clarity of observation with an exalted, inspirational space where one feels very in touch with God or something larger and greater than one's self.

VESZELVITE: Enables a Priest to be very powerful in the area in which they choose to be powerful in. Particularly empowers them in manifesting positive pole of their role; i.e., be more compassionate. For young priests, this stone has the same effect as Sphene.

LIGHT BLUE ZIRCON: Helps priests or those with priest essence twins feel very stable. Keeps the chakras open just the right amount and, thus, in balance.

ARTISAN: "Creative, innovative, unusual, spontaneous, eccentric, self-sufficient, imaginative."(I)

ACTINOLITE: (Also called Smaragdite). Enables an artisan to be very powerful in the area in which they choose to be powerful whether it's in relationships, politics or just making money. It particularly enables artisans to focus their power in the area of creativity and handle several projects at once without getting scattered or sidetracked.

AUGELITE: A productivity rock for artisans or those who are doing artistic, creative projects. Makes it easier to manifest and follow through with projects to completion. Particularly useful for mature and old artisans as they tend to go too much to seed: i.e., get lazy and fail to complete projects.

ANDESINE FELDSPAR: Balances, grounds and integrates mature and old artisans.

11

HOWLITE: Related to the 6th chakra. Pulls one into artistic creation and inspiration of a higher intellectual sort. Heals the 6th chakra. Helps one bring new things into one's life by coming up with creative ideas about it.

LLANOITE: For creativity of the "genius" sort. Promotes unusual thought patterns for the creation of highly unusual solutions to problems or fresh perspectives. An example might be that one knew there were three planes and suddenly realized there was a fourth dimension. A different way to process intellectually which can make one look eccentric when viewed from the outside.

MARIPOSITE: Empire building for sages and artisans.

BOULDER OPAL: (Opal still growing in the matrix. Blue with flashes of light). A good stone for artisans or anyone at 5th level. A truly elegant, very unusual stone that only people who have a sense of difference would appreciate. Good for working in pentangles; aids the eccentric to come up with wild and crazy ideas. Highly inspired but in a bizarre fashion: it's like a leap to a higher level of knowledge of something that pulls a lot of things together that suddenly works. Its like WOW!

SONOMA OPAL: An emotional stabilizer in general, but emotionally balancing particularly for mature artisans. Good for anyone who is pursuing a hobby, career, or artistic endeavor that requires they be creative and emotionally stable at the same time. Creates a link between the 2nd and 4th chakras and keeps them aligned; keeps one from going into manic-depressive mood swings or getting easily upset, both of which can happen when deeply involved in an artistic or creative endeavor.

PRASE or PRASIOLITE: Same in effect as Actinolite.

DARK BLUE SAPPHIRE: Pulls in creativity and enables anyone to tap into their creative potential. Opens the 2nd chakra and enables one to use it for creative purposes only. Thus, the stone feels nurturing because it allows anyone to creatively express who they really are. Helps you find creative solutions to problems when you need to. Has tendency to ground one's creativity and keep it from getting too scattered and from this standpoint, useful in follow -through. Because the dark blue Sapphire grounds the 2nd chakra (sexual center) and promotes a certain stick-to-itiveness, it is also good in relationships and will

12

create a sense of loyalty and bondedness particularly for artisans and the more fluid roles.

LILAC SAPPHIRE: (rare) Very balancing for mature and old artisans who have already learned to use their creativity but who are feeling lazy or blocked because they're in the negative pole of their chief feature. This stone allows the creativity to flow freely and intensely. Can also be used by anyone who is creatively talented and feels blocked.

SCOLECITE: Balances infant, baby and young artisans.

SAGE: **Sages are the informers, disseminators and truth-tellers. They are expressive, truthful, entertaining, humorous, verbally skillful and loving of wisdom.**

CHAROLITE: A power mode stone for sages. Helps sages feel and project an aura of confidence and authority. Not useful for other roles.

GREEN CRYSTAL: Assists communication by making a person energized and ready to communicate. Brings a sage as well as others out of withheldness and into a party-like mode and willingness to communicate.

EMERALDS: A sage stone and multi-purpose rock. Make one feel more communciative . Are extremely balancing for anyone who has to deal with communication or with processing a great deal of information , and with trying to feel out the truth the way that sages do and there is much information to sort through. Useful when feeling a great deal of confusion about "what should I do with my life" and you're trying to answer this question from several different levels at once. Balancing for high frequency, mid-range male/female energy types. Softens arrogance and self-deprecation.

OLIGOCLASE FELDSPAR: Balances, grounds and integrates mature and old sages.

YELLOW GROSSULAR: Balances infant, baby and young sages. Relates to the kinesthetic aspect of sageness. Calms sages and reduces the feeling of being overbuzzed and that they'll not be able to get all the information out. Creates the feeling that they will be able to do it all, say it all and get it all out. Very good for those in the acting professions or media. This stone doesn't work well for roles other than sage since other roles just don't get stuck in quite the same way. Good for sages who talk too much.

13

HESSONITE: (Orange-brown Grossular. Also called "Cinnamon Stone"). Balances mature and old sages. About being less buzzy, gossipy, or in the negative pole of sage; i.e., not orating or overtalking so much. Mellows out sages.

MARIPOSITE: Empire building for sages and artisans.

GREEN SPINEL: (Also called Ceylonite & Pleonaste). Sage stone. Emphasizes wisdom. Helps anyone communicate well and increases vocabulary. A general information type of rock.

GREEN to DK. GREEN TOURMALINE: (Also called Verdelite). Assists communication. Produces greater ability to communicate. Makes a sage feel they are very much themselves (very sagey). Makes anyone feel like they can be sagelike whether they are or not, i.e., be a good communicator and disseminator of information and truth.

WARRIOR: Warriors "make life work in a practical manner." They are "persuasive, good organizers and promoters, productive, energetic, resourceful and straightforward."(I)

ADAMITE: A "specificity" rock. Produces a quality of particularness. Makes you more able to see details and to proceed in a step-by-step, delineated fashion from a to b to c, etc. A warrior quality useful to other roles as well. Also, this stone helps bring you out of confusion, so it is useful for those in the negative pole of growth. It enables one to focus on the details or specifics of their situation. Also good for the exalted roles as many tend to look at whole pictures and have trouble getting down to particulars.

CASSITERITE: Enables a warrior to be very powerful in whatever area they choose. Particularly empowers warriors to be more productive and to use warrior qualities powerfully.

GARNET: (Comes in a variety of colors. Rose-red, red, and red-brown are colors specific to warriors). In general, for productivity and increased havingness.

ALMANDINE: (Red with a violet tint). For productivity: Enables one to overcome laziness and scatteredness of purpose. One feels more focused and able to get things done in a competent, purposeful fashion.

CUBIC ZIRCONIA: (All colors) Man-made garnet. Has a much stronger energy than the other garnets so a little more on the empire building side. Makes one bold, strong and

14

structured in one's productivity. Strongly warrior like.

PYROPE: (Red with brown tint). Pulls in productivity with the qualities of happiness and abundance; i.e., not just producing, but producing abundantly and having a sense of happiness at the same time.

RHODOLITE GARNETS: (Rose-red or pale violet type of pyrope). Also for productivity, but related more specifically to one's career.

STAR GARNET: (Star is formed by Rutile). The Garnet produces warrior-like productivity as described above and the star pulls in the power to back the productivity and keep it going.

HOLLANDITE: Enables a warrior to be powerful in whatever area they choose. Particularly, empowers them to feel masterful about manifesting the positive pole of their role.

HUNTITE: A productivity rock in that it clears anything excess out of the space and allows one to concentrate on just what needs to be done. Allows one to prioritize so one can productively accomplish everything.

LABRADORITE: (Also called Azulisite). Balancing for mature and old warriors. Makes a warrior feel like a warrior more than any other stone. Makes them feel energized and even if they have been over-producing or over-scheduling themselves, that they have their energy back and are healed. Useful for anyone who tends to overwork themselves--will feel re-energized.

YOUNGITE: A king and warrior stone. Produces inspiration in a moving centered way. Inspires solutions to problems requiring action on the physical plane. Energizes one to solve difficult problems.

GRAY ZOISITE: Balances infant, baby and young warriors.

KING: **Kings strive to master themselves and their environment. They are expert, gentle in nature, commanding, natural leaders and good at delegating. They are charismatic, and powerful.**

DIAMONDS: About mastery on the physical plane; i.e., situations external to one's self. Enables one to see ways to handle a situation one desires to master. Promotes a feeling of richness and abundance. Most exact and male-energied crystalline structure of all the stones so they have a very kingly and exacting quality to them, and thus useful for

feeling masterful. Certain roles resonate best with certain
colors.
    BLACK: Kings
    BLUE: Priests
    BROWN: Scholars
    CLEAR: Warriors
    GREEN: Sages
    PINK-RED: Artisans
    YELLOW: Servers
BYTOWNITE FELDSPAR: Balances, grounds and integrates
    mature and old kings.
PSILOMANE: (Also called Tiger-Eye Matrix, Tiger Iron, or
    Quartz Lignite). Enables a king to be powerful and influential
    in the area of choice be it relationships, politics, or money.
    Particularly empowering in the area of mastery or skills natural
    to kings.
SCAPOLITE: Balances mature and old kings. Useful for
    anyone in a position of power to remain balanced and to use
    power appropriately to master situations. Colors correspond
    to different races:
    PINK: Old king; black race.
    WHITE: Mature king; black, red and brown races.
    CLEAR: Old king; red and brown races.
    CAT'S EYE: Old and mature kings; oriental races.
    VIOLET: Old king; white race.
    YELLOW: Mature king; white race.
TSAVORITE: (Green) For self mastery. Produces a feeling of
    self-mastery, happiness and confidence about one's own life
    even though it may not be noticeable to others. Thus, not as
    showy as a diamond.
UNIKITE: Power: dominance: to completely and totally take
    charge of your own life. Helps protect personal power and
    not allow others to lord it over you: to be the guardian of your
    own fate and not taken over by anyone else.
WHITE ZOISITE: Balances infant, baby and young kings.

SCHOLAR: Scholars are "driven to know and
    assimilate knowledge."(I) They are curious,
    truthful, thorough, unassuming and innately
    knowledgeble though not necessarily academic.
BRAZILIANITE: Balances mature and old scholars. Pulls them
    into investigating things in incredible detail or into

16

investigating the unusual, esoteric or bizarre without getting burned out.

CORNUBITE: Creates confidence in one's ability to teach. Helps the knowledge flow forth. Useful for any role that is involved in teaching.

GOSHENITE: (Colorless Beryl). Balances infant, baby and young scholars (or an older scholar) who get into rigid, opinionated theorizing and resist any new information that might challenge the theories they've become so attached to. An anti-pigheadedness stone. Useful for anyone who gets into pontificating out of emotion or an inappropriate use of centers. Centers a person in the positive pole of intellectual center and in knowledge rather than theory.

YELLOW SAPPHIRE: Brings one directly into knowledge (what do I know and not know) and using that knowledge appropriately. Brings in the ability to memorize or retain information: the ability to really learn. Also, when one wears this stone, new opportunities start to arise; i.e., opens up options. Maintains one in the positive pole of intellectual center and makes it difficult to have opinions based on inappropriate use of the other centers.

PADPARADSCHAH: (Orange sapphire): For the scholar who is comfortable with being very powerful and is basically ready to build an empire and be in charge of the lives of many or influence the world in a big way.

IMPERIAL TOPAZ: Makes scholars feel good about themselves and reduces their tendency toward self-deprecation when involved in a project that involves use of intellect and knowledge. Makes anyone feel they will be able to exercise all their abilities and talents, that they are intelligent enough, that they have enough information and, in general, that they have enough scholarly ability to handle the situation.

BROWN ZOISITE: Balances young scholars.

NOTE: In order to understand how the Feldspars work, it is necessary to say a few words about how a person working in role operates. Each role has a favorite chakra through which they work and can be said to specialize when doing the work

17

or engaging in the functions most particular to the manifestation of their role. A lack of balance occurs when that chakra gets opened too much particularly in contrast to the other chakras who either have not changed or have closed down. What Feldspar does is keep the chakra through which the person is working at the appropriate amount of openness, in alignment with and synchronized with the other chakras.

Favorite chakras as they relate to role are:

1st: King
2nd: Artisan
3rd: Warrior
4th: Server
5th: Sage
6th: Scholar
7th: Priest

ROLES

	ORDINAL	EXALTED
	SERVER	**PRIEST**
	|Clinochlor	|Axinite
	|Clinozoisite	|Albite Feldspar
	|Cuprolite	|LT. BLUE SAPPHIRE
	|Red Feldspar	|Spene
INSPIRATION	|Heliodor	|Vanadanite
	|RUBY	|Veszelvite
	|White Sapphire		
	|Purple Spinel		
	|Sylvite		
	|Pink Zoisite		
	|Green Zoisite		
	ARTISAN	**SAGE**
	|Actinolite	|Charolite
	|Augelite	|Green Crystal
	|Andesine Feldspar	|Emerald
	|Howlite	|Oglioclase Feldspar
EXPRESSION	|Mariposite	|Yellow Grossular
	|Boulder Opal	|Hessonite
	|Sonoma Opal	|Mariposite
	|Prase or Prasiolite	|Green Spinel
	|DK BLUE SAPPHIRE	|GREEN TOURMALINE
	|Lilac Sapphire		
	|Scolecite		
	WARRIOR	**KING**
	|Adamite	|DIAMOND
	|Cassiterite	|Bytownite Feldspar
	|GARNET	|Psilomane
ACTION	|Star Garnet	|Scapolite
	|Labradorite Feldspar	|Tsavorite
	|Hollandite	|Unikite
	|Youngite	|White Zoisite
	|Gray Zoisite		

19

NEUTRAL

	SCHOLAR
	Brazilianite
	Cornubite
ASSIMILATIVE	Anorthite Feldspar
	Goshenite
	YELLOW SAPPHIRE
	Padparadschah
	Imperial Topaz
	Brown Zoisite

NOTE: For each role, there is one stone set in capital letters. This is the stone we were originally given as most reflecting the qualities of the role it is associated with.

GOALS

GOAL: "The underlying accomplishment that the
  Essence aims for in that life. It determines what
  is the bottom line issue in every experience
  during the life." (I)

GROWTH: A life with the goal of growth "is set up
  as a series of challenges and obstacles provided
  for the tempering of Essence's character and
  spiritual nature." (I). The purpose of growth is to
  evolve.

EPIDOTE: Pulls one into the positive pole of growth
  (evolution). Promotes regular and steady evolution and, at
  the same time, allows you to remain powerful while evolving.
  Epidote is also related to self-mastery in that it enables you to
  remain powerful in a situation where another would like to
  victimize you, be destructive to you in some way, or make
  you powerless. Protects the power chakra.

PERIDOT: (Also called Olivine). For growth, but very intense.
  When worn, growth escalates, the adventure box is opened
  and new challenges abound. If one is already growing very
  strongly, then wearing this stone could be overkill. Remove
  if things become crazy or challenges dangerous. Peridot is
  very good for people who are overly stagnated or in a rut as it
  will unblock them very quickly. Color varies from yellow to
  dark green. Yellow is more intense and the green is milder in
  effect. Combine with amethyst and citrine to temper the
  effect.

SINHALITE: (Yellow-brown or green-brown). Similar to Peridot:
  i.e., allows more challenges to come into one's life at a more
  rapid pace. Good if bored and one wants a little more
  excitement. Also good for those in stagnation or in growth
  who feel a little stuck and want to move ahead.

PINK ZIRCON: For astral growth. Pushes you to go out and do
  astral lessons at night instead of staying in your body or just
  wandering around the astral plane if you do leave. Astral
  lessons are emotional in nature and can result in a rather
  restless night.

RE-EVALUATION: "Re-evaluation is the opposite
   of growth in the sense that it limits the scope of
   life in such a way as to examine one or more major
   issues fully." (I)
COBALTITE: Helps one to integrate one's lessons and pull the
   various aspects into a coherent whole. Useful for those at
   the third level of any soul age and for those who either wish
   to do some reevaluation or who have a lifetime of
   reevaluation.
PINK CRYSTAL: Simplicity. Helps you recuperate from heavy
   re-evaluation or growth by pulling you into the positive pole
   of re-evaluation, thus clearing the confusion about where to
   look to see what's going on. Streamlines things; makes you
   feel like its o.k. to be more relaxed and look at things from a
   simpler point of view.
HEMATITE: (Also called Specularite). Useful when you want to
   really look something over; pulls up all stuff that needs to be
   looked at and makes it really clear what the issue is.
   Particularly good for priests (they have a tendency to go out
   into the future and miss all the middle parts) and those in
   passion mode (they tend to enthusiastically skip past things
   they need to learn). Also useful for focusing on past lives.
MARGERITE: (Looks like Rhodocrosite crystals). Takes you
   back to a state of innocence and simplicity with few
   preconceived notions about how things are. Puts you into
   taking a look at what's going on in your life without a sense of
   struggle about it. Good for cynics, skeptics, and
   over-growers.
PICTURE JASPER: Enables you to use past life, or earlier in
   this life memories, very effectively as this stone helps you
   recall the story that goes along with the issue you are
   re-evaluating. Thus, you can look at the story and
   extrapolate from there what went wrong or where you went
   off the path and what you need to do or understand about it.
MARCASITE: Similar in effect to Hematite although a little more
   gentle: i.e., kick back with your slippers and pipe and reflect
   for a while.

ACCEPTANCE: The issue for this goal is "being
   accepted by others and accepting their life and
   those in it." (I)
APATITE: (All colors). An acceptance stone that with
   continued use puts you into higher emotional centers. It

22

works by making one unconditionally accepting of things and people that come into one's life. It is almost acceptance and growth mixed because of the willingness to accept everything that could possibly flow in or a greed stone since it says "give me more" rather than less. Due to its qualities of unconditional love and acceptance, this stone is useful when you must work with or in some way accept difficult people or situations into your life. All colors have the same effect, but you will feel most comfortable with the color you resonate to best. Very potent, so a small piece will work well.

BLUE GREEN CRYSTAL: Same as blue-green tourmaline although milder in effect.

BLUE GREEN TOURMALINE: (Also called Indicolite). Wear to be more open-hearted, giving, and accepting of what's going on or of other people. One experiences more agape and is more tolerant, in general, of others. Invites people in rather than closes them out. Useful for those in impatience as it pulls one out of intolerance into tolerance.

VOLCANIC ASH: (Fused). For acceptance and surrender to the inevitable. Doesn't help you with the emotional aspects of accepting a difficult situation; e.g., working through the grief or anger. Helps you acknowledge and recognize that nothing can be done and that surrender is appropriate.

DISCRIMINATION: **The purpose of this goal is to learn to pick and choose "what one does or does not want in one's life. People with this goal develop their critical faculties and learn to express reasoned opinions on any matter of judgment."** (I)

ATACAMITE: (Green). Related to discrimination in a very specific way: it enables you to be more discriminating about new surroundings; i.e., a new job, a new house, or even a new couch. More specific than smoky quartz. Great for starting a new cycle and not accepting things you might later regret as those in acceptance are prone to do. Enables you to discriminate appropriately about structuring a new situation. Saves you the trouble of having to change the status quo later on.

CHALCEDONY: (Grey, blue & white). Discriminating in a more rejecting way than atacamite or smoky quartz. Emphasis is on what I don't want. Colors make you more discriminating in certain ways: Greyish tends to make you see what you don't want materially; the purplish color makes you see what you don't want emotionally in your life; blue goes into what you don't want intellectually in your space. The gray is usually preferred because most people prefer to clear things out of their life rather than people or ideas.

CHELSET: (Pink) Makes you more discriminating about your appearance. Useful for people who don't pay much attention to how they look. People who are intellectually or moving centered tend to ignore their appearance a lot. Makes you feel like you are taking better care of yourself which, in turn, creates a greater sense of self-esteem.

GRAY CRYSTAL: (can occur naturally). Similar to smoky quartz in the way it works, but milder and a bit more repressed. Creates clarity about whether you want this or that in your life. Because of the element of repression, it has overtones of elegance when worn.

BLUE-GREY SPINEL: Strongest discrimination stone. Enables one to reject anything out of their space: germs out of the body; people out of one's life. Wonderful for illness and super dump jobs. Paradoxically, this stone helps young, mature or old souls who have constant dealings with infant or baby souls to relate to them better. One is able to discriminate very clearly about how to behave around a baby soul and, thus, be more appropriate. Have to exercise some caution here because one can also be rejecting with this stone.

SMOKY QUARTZ: (Also called Smoky Topaz, Cairngorm or Morion). Useful when you want to work through something and reject it, or respond to a situation or person on a more discriminating basis; i.e., do I want this or do I want that. Brings in a way to cut away the dead wood and be appropriate. Wear hematite and smoky quartz to evaluate personal matters. Helps those in acceptance "clean out the garage".

BLUE TOURMALINE: (Color can range from very light to very dark blue. Also called Indicolite). Enables one to be more discriminating about the people, situations or things one wants in one's life. Helps you push the things you don't want away. Similar to Blue Spinel, but much more gentle and it doesn't help one deal with other soul ages. Makes you very clear, calm and

24

centered about what you don't want in your life. Be
careful in its use because the calm can verge on being
cold and calculating. Can use in conjunction with light
blue Sapphire (compassion) or blue-green Tourmaline
(acceptance) to soften this aspect.

WILLIAMSITE: (Bright green and black). Assists in the
appropriate use of discrimination for those with a goal
other than discrimination as it can be difficult to use
discrimination appropriately. If one is already in
discrimination, the use of this stone will probably
make them too picky.

**DOMINANCE: "For dominance, life is a win or
lose game, and people with this goal want to
win."(I) Dominance wants to lead and the
positive pole of dominance is to create a
win-win situation.**

IOLITE: (Also called Dichroite or Water Sapphire). A
very strong dominance stone. You will know you are
the one to lead and be listened to. Others will accept
it as you will be so sure of yourself. Particularly good
for the overly mushy, overly ingratiating, and overly
submissive person. Good as an anti-martyrdom stone
since it makes a person feel so confident about their
ability to take charge of their life, it is very difficult
to continue to feel that one is a victim of the
circumstances. Different colors affect different
areas of one's life.
BLUE: Dominance in friendships.
GRAY: Dominance in career.
PURPLE: (Also called Cordierite). Dominance in
sexual and familial relationships.

BLUE TOPAZ: Puts you more in control of a situation,
able to competently lead and dominate. People look at
you and respect your leadership qualities. Not as
heavy in its effect as iolite. Makes it more like you
can be very competent and a leader and be proud.
Makes you seem more competent rather than
dominating. Wear for meeting with the IRS.

VESUVIANITE: Helps one to compete, to come from a

25

desire to win, and to be appropriate with one's competitiveness. Encourages a "win-win" attitude rather than one of tromping on the competition.

SUBMISSION: "A goal which allows an Essence to be devoted to a cause or totally supportive of another person or group of people." (I)

KUNZITE: Makes you feel you could surrender to whatever is happening; that you can handle it; that you can accept something that's out of your control and surrender to it. It is not the devotional form of submission. Very useful because people spend so much time resisting things that are truly out of their control. Michael regards this as one of the most useful of rocks and recommends it highly.

PINK SAPPHIRE: (Light to medium pink color). Brings out one's ability to surrender to a cause or another person for the greater good. It is a delegation and surrender stone. Allows one to go with or surrender to people who can handle things better than you can. Can also be really devotional and appreciative of the people who are doing those things: i.,e., that you have surrendered to. Will tone down dominance and aggression and let life flow more. Also allows things "not in control" to be more acceptable. A very people-oriented stone.

PINK SPINEL: (Pink to red in color). An other-oriented stone: submission and devotion to those you love. Enables one to surrender to and be devoted to another person. Can set one's ego aside when with them and be loving even when its tough. A good wedding ring stone.

WOODHOUSITE: Makes you feel you can submit to the greater good. Easier to surrender and not be so much in control.

STAGNATION: "The purpose of having stagnation as a goal is to take a 'rest' life and to learn how to 'go with the flow'."(I)

MESOLITE: "Go with the flow" rock. Similar to Pink Tourmaline. Pulls one into the positive pole of stagnation and allows one to be more free-flowing. Particularly good for those who are over-stressed or who work too hard, as it would enable them to relax somewhat; allow themselves to be less stressed and stop putting boulders in the middle of their own stream. A "let's go on vacation" rock; totally relax and detoxify. Can move immediately into a restful state instead of taking several days to wind down.

PINK TOURMALINE: (Also called Rubellite or Siberite or Uvite). Enables one to go with rather than resist the normal flow of one's life; i.e, not surrendering, but going with the flow in the direction of least resistance in terms of what one wants to get out of the situation. Good to wear when you take a week off; makes you very relaxed and is particularly good if you have a difficult time unwinding. Do not use when you want to be dynamic and out there in the world accomplishing things.

GOALS

	ORDINAL	EXALTED
INSPIRATION	RE-EVALUATION |Cobaltite |HEMATITE |Picture Jasper |MARCASITE |Margerite |Pink Crystal	GROWTH |Epidote |PERIDOT |Sinhalite |Pink Zircon | |
EXPRESSION	DISCRIMINATION |Atacamite |Blu/Gray Chalcedony |Chelset |Grey Crystal |Blue/Gray Spinel |SMOKY QUARTZ |BLUE TOURMALINE |Williamsite	ACCEPTANCE |Apatite |BLUE-GREEN | TOURMALINE |Blue-Green Crystal |Volcanic Ash | | |
ACTION	SUBMISSION |Kunzite |PINK SAPPHIRE |Pink Spinel |Woodhousite	DOMINANCE |Iolite |BLUE TOPAZ |Vesuvianite |

	NEUTRAL
ASSIMILATIVE	STAGNATION |Mesolite |PINK TOURMALINE

MODES

MODE: "The method or action one takes to achieve one's goal."(2) One's "modus operandi" in life.

REPRESSION: The positive pole of repression mode involves a sense of restraint, containment, discipline and refinement.

ALEXANDRITE: Repression mode. Inhibits others from coming into your space. Limits them and inhibits the elements you don't want around, particularly when worn on the power hand (left). Also inhibits cording. Alexandrite produces emotional inhibition when worn on the chest: when worn in the ears, it inhibits or restricts ability of the higher intellectual center. It is a sophisticated stone as it also brings life to the more refined and elegant side.

EUCLASE: Pulls one into a state of striving for excellence and trying to achieve perfection. One wants to be exactly correct on all levels. Good to wear when you want to make an incredibly good impression. Or, if you need to deal with very difficult people in a difficult situation, it will help you remain diplomatic and tactful.

GIMELINITE: (Beige Crystalls). Increases the delicacy of one's movements and aura of refinement in general.

TANTALITE: Helps those in respression slide to passion mode.

PASSION: The positive pole of passion mode is experienced as being intensely alive, very involved and enthusiastic and self actualizing.

CORAL; WHITE TO RED: Wear to create emotional openness and enthusiasm. The effect of coral is more intense the redder the stone. Goes well with dark green tourmaline for communication.

APPLE CORAL: Also passion mode, but related to the emotional part of the instinctive center. The result is that one is very deeply caring and warm-hearted about people; open to loving and being involved with others and, at the same time, healed of fear about such closeness.

29

CAUTION: In the positive pole of caution mode, one proceeds in a deliberate, careful fashion, taking one's time and avoiding any risks or dangers.

CITRINE: Use when you want to slow things down, when you want to create a steady pace or when you want to put the brakes on. Provides a sense of stability especially when things are moving too quickly. Citrine also builds up your stamina and makes it easier to keep going through difficult processes or karmas. Color varies from light yellow to orange. The mildest effect is with the lightest color. Good combined with power mode stones or Peridot as it makes the use of power or the process of growth steady and predictable rather than impulsive. Also useful for the hyperkinetic or those super high-energy folks who can't seem to calm down or slow down.

POWER: The positive pole of power mode projects an aura of strength and authority. A person in power mode is very noticeable and their presence very commanding.

AQUAMARINE: Helps project an aura of real strength particularly when you're not sure you are that strong. Makes others pay attention to you even though you may not believe in yourself. Pulls you into power mode and helps you take command especially in situations when you have to act powerfully. Helps adjust to being authoritative and in control without feeling wishy-washy about it.

PIEMONTITE EPIDOTE: (Cherry red in color). Very powerful stone. Good for getting people motivated, feeling empowered and ready to go. Makes you feel like you're pulsing with power and "get up and go" energy. A good cure for laziness.

RUTILLATED QUARTZ: Pulls you into being powerful and being clear with regard to what you're being powerful about. You not only look very clear and capable of handling everything, but you feel that way as well.

VARISCITE: Power and winning. A combination of power and being balanced between dominance and submission. You want to win and you want other people to win and you can see what it is that pulls it all together so there will be a winning

30

solution for everyone. You feel you are the power backing that up and that you can make it happen. The feeling you can come up with winning solutions increases self-confidence.

PRESERVERANCE: In the positive pole of perserverance, one has a great deal of perserverance, staying power and stick-to-itiveness.

JAMESONITE: For stability, security and steadfastness. Helps you perservere through very long, even life-long tasks. Makes you feel grounded and secure that you can perservere over very long periods of time regardless of what comes up. A very hard-working rock.

WATERMELON TOURMELINE (BI-COLOR PINK & GREEN): Perserverance mode. Gives others the impression you are stable, reliable and count-on-able whether you are or not. It also enables one to draw on those qualities to the extent one possesses them. Helps very fluid types manifest their solidity and very female energied types manifest their male energy.

OWYHEE JASPER: A combination of Uranian Agate (eccentric body type energy), bright red Jasper (aggressive energy and dynamism), and a pale yellow to green Jasper. The pale green is an aggresson calmer, so the entire combo would put you in perserverance mode with the Uranian Agate adding a higher intellectual or unique, eccentric way of looking at your problems. Useful to have around if there is something you need to deal with dynamically, but not too aggressively, for a long time, and be able to come up with unusual solutions for problems that are not easily solveable. Good to combine with Green Jade for tranquility and harmony.

AGGRESSION: Those in the positive pole of aggression are very dynamic, adventurous and risk-taking and assertive.

CINNABAR: Aggression mode. Enables you to be dynamic and enhances everything that aggression mode entails. Good for those who are too meek and mild or who have overleaves that are a little too submissive. Warriors are very attracted to this stone although they usually do not need it, i.e.,.they have mastered the qualities this stone enhances.

RED CRYSTAL: Same qualities as Cinnabar but much milder in its effect. In general, makes you more dynamic and lively.

FIRE OPAL & FIRE AGATE: Aggression mode. Use when you want to be powerful in a particular circumstance such as teaching an unfamiliar class. This stone allows one to project an incredible charisma so if you are already strong, use the power with care. The effect is less intense with a timid or unpowerful person: the action would be to make them feel able to operate effectively in the world.

RED JASPER: (True red in color). Produces a dynamic and lively energy. In general is a good stone for balancing the energy centers of the body.

OBSERVATION: In the positive pole, one's observations are very clear, sharp and insightful.

CLEAR CRYSTAL: For clarity of observation. The clearer the stone, the better for observation. Crystals have a special quality in that they are very individual and a particular person will resonate to one but not to another. Man-made crystals (leaded crystal) although milder in effect are also good observation stones but have no individual character: no "pet rock" feeling. Crystals produce clarity in whatever way they are used and this clarity does not have to be visual. For example, if placed on a chakra, that chakra will become clear and thus more energized.

DIASPORE: For clarity of observation. More observing about what is going on with you personally: about you and what you're up to; what may be effective or not be effective. Makes you look within and see what you've been ignoring. Doesn't dig up instinctive issues.

GEODES (THUNDER EGGS): Observation. Each thunder egg represents a different observation about something that's so: i.e., reminds you of a particular observation that you've made. You will be attracted to the Geode that represents the observation you wish to stay aware of. For example, one might remind you that you need to exercise since you have observed that you need to exercise. Tends to encapsulate a certain observation for a certain person.

HERKIMER DIAMOND: Combines the clarity of quartz with mastery energy because of the double-edged shape. Good for vivid dreaming and astral clarity. With Rhodocrosite, would help you remember your dreams.

SNOW QUARTZ: An observation stone. When snowy in color rather than clear, one moves into childlikeness: innocence dominates the observations: no adult cynical viewpoints are in the way of one's observations. Can observe from a place of innocence--fresh and clear in the sense of not much preconceived stuff. Good balancing stone for children. Helps them be clear about the world and be comfortable in a child body. Sages are attracted to Snow Quartz because sages grow up at a slow rate and often feel like their bodies are maturing at a faster rate than they are.

MODES

	ORDINAL	EXALTED
INSPIRATION	**REPRESSION** |ALEXANDRITE |Euclase |Gimelinite |Tantalite	**PASSION** |CORAL |Apple Coral | |
EXPRESSION	**CAUTION** |CITRINE | | |	**POWER** |AQUAMARINE |Piemontite Epidoe |Rutillated Quartz |Variscite
ACTION	**PRESERVERE** |Jamesonite |Owyhee Jasper |WATERMELON | TOURMALINE	**AGGRESSION** |CINNABAR |Red Crystal |Fire Opal |Fire Agate

NEUTRAL

ASSIMILATIVE	**OBSERVATION** |CLEAR CRYSTAL | |Diaspore | |Geodes | |Herkimer Diamond | |Snow Quartz |

ATTITUDES

ATTITUDE: "The primary perspective: the stance
from which we look at things; how we go about
deciding what to do."(2) A basic point of view.

STOIC: In the positive pole, stoics manifest
tranquility, emanate calm, peace and harmony."(2)
They reserve their emotions and are stable.
GREEN JADE: (Also called Nephrite. Darkish green, mossy in
color). Produces a tranquil attitude. Good when depressed.
More able to be resigned to difficult or unpleasant aspects of
your life you cannot avoid; a situation in life you simply have
to handle. You may not ever be happy with it and, the
situation itself may always be somewhat stressful, but this
stone will make you feel more grounded and capable of
dealing with the situation.

SPIRITUALIST: The spiritualist is visionary, is able
to see the variety of possibilities inherent in a
situation and enjoys "pursuits of a philosophical
nature." (2)
HAMBERGITE: Pulls one into a spiritualistic, utopian
viewpoint: i.e., really inspired by utopian concepts and the
wonderful possibilities in the universe. Has to do with
fomenting ideas rather than manifesting them.
PAKISTAN JADE: Puts you in touch with spiritualist energy
and enables one to come up with some great, wild ideas.
Similar to Hambergite.
PINK HALITE: For the spiritualist. Pulls you into higher
intellectual center. One feels visionary and larger than self
and, in that sense, inspired.
MOONSTONE: Opens up a person with tunnel vision (i.e.,
only able to see one goal and one way of achieving it). Helps
you get what you want by seeing more clearly the
possibilities of life or a situation.
SOUTHERN JADE: (Nephrite that has been heat treated. Dark
rust-red in color). Pulls gently into spiritualism from stoicism.

35

SKEPTIC: The skeptic likes to investigate matters and consider all aspects of a situation: does not believe in anything, and strives for knowledge.

ORANGE JADE: For skepticism. Useful when you're not sure of your value out there in the world; i.e., are you being suckered or not. Helps you be less gullible and naive about what's actually so. Good with the scholar stone (Golden Sapphire) for people who are fuzzy and naive.

IDEALIST: The idealist can see how things could be ideally; combines the best of all possibilities into a unified whole to produce coalescence.

ACCANTITE: Helps one be more idealistic especially when they're not an idealist. Makes you feel more optimistic in general.

LAVENDER JADE: For idealism. Useful when you feel you're being too cynical and unimaginative. Not for someone fuzzy as it would make them feel it was just fine to remain fuzzy. Skeptics like it because it puts them in an optimistic mood.

CYNIC: The cynic is able to see all the possible pitfalls or contradictions inherent in a situation; good at constructive criticism and "questioning commonly held beliefs."(2)

BLACK CALCITE: Allows you to look at things in the worst possible light if that's what you feel you need to do. Can see everything that could possibly go wrong. Thus, can take precautions or work all possible problems through instead of passing them over.

JET: For cynicism. Wear when necessary to go into a situation with eyes open; e.g., being in a war where its useful to keep self in survival mode, or in business where much back biting occurs or when being undermined, or in a hassle with someone who wants to bring about a disaster for you.

PEROVSKITE: Increases cynicism in a person who is too gullible.

36

REALIST: The realist is able to see a situation
  objectively and realistically.
BENJAMININTE with AIKINITE: (Thin Silver metal on
  Quartz). Helps one to be realistic about the
  possibilities in the present and in the near future.
BURNITE: Helps one stay very realistic especially when
  worried about one's ability to see things objectively
  and remain neutral in a situation. Helps you see
  clearly what there is to see without feeling too drawn
  to be either too pessimistic or too optimistic.
WHITE JADE: For realism. Makes it easy to perceive
  objective reality. Good for people who float out of
  their bodies a lot. Can have an extremely calming
  effect for those who usually can't tell what's going on.
  White Jade makes them feel grounded and that they
  know what's really so.

PRAGMATIST: The pragmatist is practical,
  efficient, and a sensible rule maker.
GOLDEN TOPAZ: Useful for knowing what procedures
  will work in a particular situation. Enables one to
  delineate steps A, B, & C without wasting time. Good
  with Garnets as this combination will pull in practical
  ways of being productive.

ATTITUDES

	ORDINAL	EXALTED
INSPIRATION	**STOIC** |GREEN JADE | | | |	**SPIRITUALIST** |Hambergite |Pakistan Jade |Pink Halite |MOONSTONE |Southern Jade
EXPRESSION	**SKEPTIC** |ORANGE JADE |	**IDEALIST** |Accantite |LAVENDAR JADE
ACTION	**CYNIC** |Black Calcite |JET | |	**REALIST** |Benjaminite with | Aikinite |Burnite |WHITE JADE

NEUTRAL

PRAGMATIST |GOLDEN TOPAZ |	| |

CENTERS: A Brief Discussion

The purpose of this discussion is to enable you to use the information in this section without needing to refer to other texts to define the terms used. This is not meant to be a complete discussion of centers as the topic is actually quite complex. If you are interested in exploring the subject in more depth, please refer to the sources listed in the bibliography.

A chakra is an energy center which has a physical location in the physical body, but is not of the physical body. The gemstones that relate to the chakras are very strong in their energy and are very noticeable. A center is the psychological or experiential component of that chakra. In this teaching, all chakras are of equal importance. There is a positive and negative pole or way of manifestation to each. In the discussion of each center, only the positive pole is discussed as gemstones only produce positive effects.

Optimally, all chakras are aligned (synchronized with each other), in balance (neither too open or too closed) and functioning normally (none shut down or ignored). Notice also the location of the three higher centers. Two are at the top of the head (6th and 7th chakras) and a third is located in the lower part of the body (2nd chakra). Michael says this is so higher centered energy can flow throughout the body.

Below is a chart which shows each chakra and the center it corresponds to. Each role also has a favorite chakra through which they work. If you know your role, it is valuable to use the chakra gemstone that corresponds to your role as it is very easy to overuse a favorite chakra. This will enable you to use your "favorite chakra" in a more appropriate and balanced fashion.

39

CENTER	CHAKRA	LOCATION	ROLE
Instinctive	First	Base of Spine	King
Higher Kinesthetic	Second	Above Sex Organs	Artisan
Kinesthetic	Third	Solar Plexus	Warrior
Emotional	Fourth	Heart	Server
Intellectual	Fifth	Throat	Sage
Higher Intellectual	Sixth	Third Eye	Scholar
Higher Emotonal	Seventh	Top of Head	Priest

Another set of terms you will encounter refer, for example, to the Messianic Plane. This is based on the explanation we have received from Michael on how the universe is structured. There are seven basic planes of existence and certain types of lessons to be learned on each plane. We are on the physical plane which is the first plane and Michael is on the Causal plane which is the third. When it is said that a certain mineral connects you with, say, the Messianic Plane, that means the energy of that plane moves through you. In this way, the gemstones are an aid to experiencing the energy of the higher centers. Below is a chart which outlines this concept.

PLANES OF EXISTENCE

Physical Plane:
    Physical lessons

Astral Plane:
    Emotional lessons

Causal Plane:
    Intellectual lessons

Mental Plane: Higher
    Intellectual Lessons
    Lao Tsu representative

Messianic Plane: Higher
    Emotional lessons
    Jesus is representative

Buddhaic Plane: Higher
    Kinesthetic lessons
    Buddha representative.

As we go through out daily life, we operate out of three centers: the intellectual, the emotional and the kinesthetic or moving center. We do not stay in or operate out of the higher centers, but can visit them if we learn how and this is commonly experienced as very enlightening (see above).

In this teaching, each person has a certain type of centering. One is either intellectually, emotionally or moving centered. This means that in encountering any given situation one's first impulse will be either to think about the situation, feel about the situation, or do something about the situation. Then each person has a second centering they go to next which is referred to as the "part of". Thus, one's centering can be the moving part of the intellectual center. This means the person will think first, act second and feel something when it is all over.The center remaining is the one used least and when a person is unbalanced is totally ignored. Instinctive centering is very rarely chosen and those who do choose this centering are regarded by our society as being insane.

You may wonder "On what basis is a gemstone or a mineral classed as a 'chakra rock'?" The gemstones listed in this section work specifically through one chakra or, sometimes, a combination of chakras. Gemstones and minerals listed else where affect the body in a general, overall fashion.

Gemstones can be used to help you emphasize any center you feel you need or want to. If you are unbalanced, choose a stone for the center you use least to get you moving through all three centers again. You will notice some gemstones enhance the qualities of a particular center and others heal that center or keep it balanced. With a little practice you will notice which work best for you. It is always wise to have a few instinctive center stones around since they keep us balanced and out of our survival issues. It is also useful to note that the gemstones affect most strongly the part of the body they are placed closest to.

CENTERS

EMOTIONAL CENTER: About feeling states such as happiness, grief or anger and the ability to be emotionally perceptive.

AURICHALCITE: For stress-related emotional healing. Particularly useful when one has taken some real hard knocks emotionally and the emotional center (heart chakra) needs healing.

RED CALCITE: (pink to salmon in color). Keeps the fourth chakra open and makes it feel protected and not so vulnerable; that its okay to open up--any negativity that one encounters will be flushed right out. Negative emotions are drained out of body rather than held or absorbed. Emotional part of the emotional center.

HETEROSITE: Emotional openness. Puts you in touch with your emotional center and opens up the emotions. Most useful for people who are emotionally blocked.

HORN: Balancing to the emotional center. Makes you feel connected to other live, warm things and that, in general, one is loved. Relates to the moving part of the emotional center.

LAPIS LAZULI: (Also called Lazulite). Balances the emotional center and enhances neutral emotional perceptivity. Not useful for calming down when one feels over emotional as this stone does not affect the type of emotion felt or its intensity. It allows one to perceive emotional issues more clearly. Intellectual part of the emotional center.

ROSASITE: (Looks like Turquoise). Most useful when one is stuck in the negative pole of the emotional center; i.e., experiencing negative emotions. This stone helps by enabling one to move forward into an appropriate action or thought that shifts the emotional reaction. Good for those who are emotionally centered as they most often get trapped in this manner.

GREEN or BLUE SMITHSONITE: Makes it easier to experience your emotions, particularly if you've been emotionally blocked.

VICTORIA STONE: Pulls more energy to the fourth chakra which stimulates the emotional center. This brings up strong emotions: they can be either positive or negative depending on what you're in the mood for.

HIGHER EMOTIONAL: Unconditional Love.

BERRYLIUM: (Lilac colored) Connects one with the Messianic Plane.

WHITE CALCITE: (Also called ICELAND SPAR). Connects one with the Messianic Plane and enables one to operate out of a feeling of love and connnectedness with the universe. Keeps the seventh chakra open and gives a feeling of protection; i.e., safe to operate out of higher centers. Also, one feels clear that one is very loving and worthy of being loved by the supreme being and worthy of being connected to and experiencing higher planes of existence.

CHRYSOCOLLA: Crystallizes feelings of higher-centered unconditional love, acceptance and tolerance toward specific others. Makes it possible to forgive others their wrongdoings toward you and be very loving and understanding out of one's abililty to see clearly who they are. Clarity of crystal is important: the clearer the crystal, the clearer ones perceptions of others are. An outward directed stone. One is very perceptive and clear about others, but not necessarily about the self.

CHRYSOPRASE: (Also called Green Chalcedony). Very similar in both chemical composition and function to chrysocolla. A little more inward focused stone. One asks: "How can I be more loving and understanding and forgiving of this other person?" While one is still very perceptive about others, clarity not quite as sharp as with Chrysocolla. Clarity of stone also very crucial with Chrysoprase. This stone is especially inspiring to artisans.

EILAT: (Blend of Chrysocolla, Turquoise and Malachite). The Malachite keeps one balanced and better able to use the higher-centered energies of the Chrysocolla and Turquoise.

HIDDENITE: (Green Spodumene). Connects one with the Messianic Plane or Buddhaic Plane.

LARAMAR: For eternal love. Allows you to keep on loving wherever you've been loving. Also makes the wearer feel emotionally supported. Very useful when a relationship is undergoing a stress and you feel your love may be jeopardized. Laramar ensures that the love that's underneath all that stuff will still be there. Also good for divorce or splits in a relationship where both would like to remain friends.

TURQUOISE: Creates a feeling of higher centered emotional connectedness and love. Not connected to specific persons like Chrysocolla and Chrysoprase. Turquoise doesn't make you look at anything.

PARROT-WING JASPER: (Combination of Chrysocolla, Turquoise & Malachite). See Eilat.

INTELLECTUAL CENTER: About conceptualizing, thinking, gaining insight and communicating it.

AMBER: Good for mental clarity. Pulls one away from emotional and moving centered energy into an intellectual focus. Good for a confused person in growth. Amber puts greatest intellectual focus near the center it is worn closest to. If worn at the 5th chakra, more intellectual in communication. If worn at the 4th chakra, intellect guides the emotional center. In general, promotes intellectual centering.

RED AMBER: Enables operation of the intellectual center by containing or deleting negative emotion: keeps you from being emotional and is calming. Related to the intellectual center by default as it keeps other influences out of the picture.

DATOLITE: (Clear or green). Produces clearer thinking.

GYPSUM: For intellectual clarity and competency. Certain colors work best for certain roles.

CHAMPAGNE: King
CLEAR: Scholar
GREEN: Sage
LT. BROWN: Warrior
WHITE: Artisans
YELLOW: Server
YELLOW-GREEN: Priest

BRECCHIATED JASPER: Heals mental stress. Centers you intellectually and makes it easier to be logical, clear headed and clear thinking. Wakes you up and increases your intellectual capacity.

BROWN SMITHSONITE: Pulls you to the fifth chakra and makes you more intellectually centered.

WHITE TOPAZ: Opens up the intellectual center and allows

44

one to maintain a clear, intellectual focus. Similar in effect to Amber.

YELLOW, BROWN & CLEAR TOURMALINE: Assists in intellectual processing.

HIGHER INTELLECTUAL: Truth and wisdom.

BROWN or GOLD CALCITE: Connects one with the mental plane. Enhances capacity to know what is true. Better able to appreciate such philosophers as Lao Tsu.

BROWN CRYSTAL: Makes one feel more open in the sixth chakra. Mild in effect. Puts one in the space of thinking.

HOWLITE: Heals the sixth chakra. Pulls one into artistic creation and inspiration. Helps one bring new things into one's life in a creative way. Artisans, in particular, like this stone.

KYANITE: Connects one to the Causal Plane. This connection not of interest usually unless one has a teacher on that plane. Michael is a causal plane teacher and those who wish to connect with them will find this stone useful.

OPALITE: Pulls excess energy in the body up and out. Particularly useful for those who tend to stay in their heads and overuse the intellectual centers.

PEARLS: Wisdom. Each Pearl is a different inspirational thought and the energies don't blend. The more misshapen the pearl, the more eccentric the thought. Such Pearls are called baroque.

BIWA PEARLS: (Fresh water Pearls). Same as Pearls but more for eccentric thought.

PURPLE SMITHSONITE: Pulls you to the sixth chakra and makes it easier to use psychic abilities.

KINESTHETIC CENTER: Also referred to as the moving center and is about moving the body; i.e., walking, dancing, crocheting or just fidgeting. Center for power issues.

BRONZITE: (Metallic green-brown). Stimulates one to exercise. Relates to the moving part of the moving center.

DUFTITE: Makes it easier to learn any skill that involves the moving center-the mechanics of the body. This includes, for example, basketweaving, car repair, woodcarving and football.

45

GRAY JASPER: Protects and heals the third chakra. Makes it easier to own one's own personal power and feel your power cannot be taken from you.

NEPTUNITE: Protects and heals the third chakra. Same in function as gray jasper.

SPECTROLITE: (BLUE TIGER EYE. Also called Hawk's eye or Falcon's Eye). Functions similarly to the White Opal though is even more powerful in its effect. Stimulates one to exercise. Makes you feel like hopping and skipping around. Moving part of the moving center.

WHITE OPAL: Makes you feel like you can use the moving center more and be productive. Energizes the body and makes you feel like getting a lot done--get up and get moving. Intellectual part of the moving center.

PURPURITE: Keeps the moving center balanced.

YELLOW SMITHSONITE: Makes you more moving centered and ready for action.

RED TIGER EYE: Gives the moving center a break. One can get too hyper or buzzed in a moving centered or physical way. Red Tiger Eye slows the third chakra down and flushes the excess energy out.

HIGHER KINESTHETIC: Beauty and perfection of physical form. A sense of connectedness and oneness with the Universe. Can be experienced through sex.

PLUME AGATE: Opens up second chakra and the expression of sexuality and creativity. Enables one to be more open sexually and less repressed. Plume Agate also helps one to express creativity more and get past the tendency to be shy and hide one's talents. Emotional part of the sexual center.

JOAQUINITE: Healing to the second chakra.

KAMMERERITE: Connects one with the Buddhaic Plane. Gives one a sense of being at peace, a sense of harmony and connectedness with the whole and at one.

LEPIDOLITE: Connects one with the Buddhaic Plane. Same as Kammererite.

BLACK OPAL: Makes one feel energetically connected to the whole. One really resonates to and is very attractive to other people especially sexually. One is very likely to be corded when wearing this stone. A very energizing stone.

JELLY OPAL: Functions the same as the Black Opal although

it is not quite as powerful.

SODALITE: Balances and increases the energy of the second chakra. Very healing when the second chakra has been overused or too shut down. Increases ones sexuality, sexual attractiveness and creativity.

INSTINCTIVE CENTER: Is responsible for automatic, autonomic functions. Contains memories of all past experiences and conflicts. Center for survival issues.

ABALONE: Healing to the instinctive center. One feels calmer and less afraid. Particularly calming to high frequency, "buzzy" types of people who live in a very intense state. Also very useful for those who have exalted roles, goals and/or attitudes.

AMIANTH: (Green and white web). Opens the instinctive center very quickly and very widely. Useful for those who need to do instinctive center work and are very shut down.

CAMEO SHELL: Good for eliminating bad habits. Opens the instinctive center and allows one to look at whether they need to keep the habit around any more. Allows evaluation of the usefulness of any particular habit.

LEOPARDSKIN AGATE: Very grounding and healing when dealing with heavy emotional issues. Reduces free-floating anxiety; i.e., when you're worried and anxious, but don't know why. Good for anyone, but also grounding for people who are paranoid or schizophrenic and those who are totally unstable and cannot handle life.

  A stone used for centuries. Called Wolfstone at one time because unconsciously it was recognized that the wolf is directly related to, and the symbol for, the emotional part of the instinctive center. Thus, this stone puts you in touch with any instinctive terrors or fears so you can work on them and conquer them.

BLUE AVENTURINE: (Also called Siderite or Blue Quartz). Keeps the first chakra and the feet open and unblocked so energy can flow through unimpeded. Varies in color from light to very dark blue.

BENJANINITE: (Orange Crystals). Heavy duty instinctive center healer and anesthetic: like pouring a gelatinous bandage over the instinctive center. Useful when one has seen or participated in very traumatic circumstances such as

47

murder, rape, or war. Later on, when numbing is no longer appropriate and when one is ready to process the experience, this stone can be put aside and another instinctive center healer chosen.

BONE: Healing and calming to the instinctive center. Same in its effect as Ivory except Ivory has a more refined quality to it. Bone makes you feel very grounded in your body. When wearing Bone, what you do will make a lot of sense and you won't be operating from fear.

BLACK CORAL: Major healer of instinctive centered fear. Importance of this is that there are two basic emotions in the universe--fear and love--when one is healed of fear, what is left is love. High frequency types might feel it drags them down to too low of a frequency; others will love it as it will feel to them that it takes the heat off. Black Coral relates to the intellectual part of the instinctive center. It heals fears by helping one to examine what's going on; i.e., opens the instinctive center and brings up instinctive material to process. This includes past lives.

APPLE CORAL: Calms instinctive fears. Creates a feeling of enthusiasm for life and is related to the emotional part of the instinctive center. Also see passion mode.

FLINT: (Also called Chert). Heals one of survival fears. Good when one has had very difficult survival experiences. Makes you feel like you can survive no matter what.

GRAY-BLACK GROSSULAR: Heals the instinctive center. Particularly good when facing survival issues such as the loss of a job. Functions similarly to bone.

IVORY: Strong instinctive healer. Helps to calm basic fears about survival whether issue is real or not. Makes one feel that survival is not an issue. When worn at the fourth chakra, one's emotions will not be coming from survival. When worn at the sixth chakra, produces inspiration about ways to solve survival issues. Relates to the moving part of the instinctive center.

BROWN or GREY JADE: (Also called butterfat jade). Very relaxing as it drains excess energy from all chakras out through the first chakra. When worn during the day, keeps excess energy from building up and helps one operate from a relaxed state.

MORRISON RANCH JASPER: Useful in doing instinctive center work such as past-life regressions. Helps bring instinctive issues to the surface and makes one feel more comfortable handling them. Also see Shamanism and Change.

LAWSONITE: Calms instinctive fears. Same in effect as Leopard Skin Agate.

LUDLAMITE: (Olive-green crystals). Very calming to the instinctive center particularly when it is "blasted." When the instinctive center has been severly taxed, one can behave in some rather bizarre ways that society would label "crazy" or "insane." This rock is strong enough to calm instinctive centers that have been that severely stresssed but, of course, it is also useful for more normal stresses to the instinctive center.

MOTHER OF PEARL SHELL: Same in effect as abalone except it is more useful for those with ordinal modes, goals, and attitudes. Very strong instinctive healer. Moving part of the instinctive center.

BLACK OBSIDIAN: Same in effect as Leopard Skin Agate.

PETRIFIED WOOD: Calms instinctive fears. Extremely grounding. Makes one feel they are a part of agelessness; nothing could go wrong. You're going to last forever.

SCHEELITE: Balances and opens the first chakra. Good because the first chakra is often closed down.

TIGILLITE: (Fossilized worm tunnels). Heals the instinctive center.

CENTER COMBINATIONS

ARAGONITE: Keeps chakras four, five and six in balance and operating in a blended fashion. This enables one to have an emotional focus, an intellectual focus and combine that with the psychic ability of the sixth chakra. Thus, one simultaneously operates from a high degree of emotional perceptivity, intellectual clarity and the ability to see truth from a higher perspective and psychically sense the flow of things. Prevents one from being over-emotional or too dry intellectually. This stone will not be very attractive to those who like a lot of drama in their life or who are uncomfortable feeling very truthful.

GREEN AVENTURINE: Keeps sixth and seventh chakras open and unblocked so energy can flow unimpeded. Green aventurine particularly good for those who have been viewed as abnormal by the culture such as those who are very high female energied (i.e., flaky) or those who are very high male energied (very focused and often scary particularly when

49

combined with a low frequency). Feeling abnormal makes it more difficult to keep the sixth and seventh chakras open and operate out of universal truth and love--more of a tendency to shut down and operate out of a sense of survival (instinctive center).

RED AVENTURINE: (Varies in color from red to peach to brown). Keeps second, third, fourth and fifth chakras open and unblocked so energy can flow unimpeded. Very important and powerful stone.

BENITOITE: Healing to the chakras. Is often found in very small pieces, but very powerful in effect so a large piece is not necessary. Benitoite comes in a variety of colors and each color is related to a different chakra and is most effective healing that chakra.

WHITE: First chakra
PINK: Fourth chakra
CLEAR: Fifth chakra
BLUE: Sixth chakra
PURPLE: Seventh chakra

BLUE CALCITE: Opens, heals and unblocks all chakras. Very intense and rapid in its effect. Similar to the aventurines although the latter operate more slowly and are gentler in effect.

GALENA: A truth stone. Aids in telling the truth and in looking for what's true. Operates through the fifth and sixth chakras.

BLACK JADE: Balances the lower three chakras which involve survival, sex and power. It integrates the lower three chakras so one is appropriate with all three. Good to wear when you want to open up, but feel attacked or that survival is an issue.

SEPTARIAN NODULE: (Combination of Aragonite, Brown Calcite, & Concretions. Concretions are naturally occurring concrete). This combination enhances the ability to perceive higher truth and love. It is energizing and keeps the energy moving throughout the body. The concretions are full of Divas and can be used by your spirit guides as a base from which to get in touch with you. Makes you more powerful because you have their energy behind you.

SMITHSONITE: (Also called Bonamite). Smithsonite comes in several colors. Each color works on a different center. In general, the effect is to pull you into functioning from a particular chakra and to clear that chakra of any blockage.

GREEN or BLUE: Makes it easier to experience your emotions particularly if you've been emotionally blocked.

50

PURPLE: Pulls you to the sixth chakra and makes it easier to use psychic abilities.

BROWN: Pulls you to the fifth chakra and makes you more intellectually centered.

YELLOW: Makes you more moving centered and ready for action.

PINK: Helps make children more psychic. Can also be used by adults, but more useful for children.

CENTERS

	ORDINAL	EXALTED
INSPIRATION	**INTELLECTUAL** |AMBER |Red Amber |Datolite |Gypsum |Brecchiated Jasper |White Topaz |Yellow, Brown & | Clear Tourmaline	**HI INTELLECTUAL** |Brown/Gold Calcite |Brown Crystal |Howlite |Opalite |PEARLS |Fresh Water Pearl | |
EXPRESSION	**EMOTIONAL** |Aurichalcite |Red Calcite |Heterosite |Horn |LAPIS LAZULI |Rosasite |Victoria Stone | |	**HI EMOTIONAL** |Beryllium |White Calcite |Crysocolla |Chrysoprase |Eilat |Hiddenite |TURQUOISE |Laramar |Parrot-Wing Jasper
ACTION	**KINESTHETIC** |Bronzite |Duftite |Gray Jasper |Neptunite |Blue Tiger Eye |WHITE OPAL |Purpurite |Red Tiger Eye	**HI KINESTHETIC** |Plume Agate |Joaquinite |Kammererite |Lepidolite |BLACK OPAL |JELLY OPAL |Sodalite |

52

NEUTRAL

ASSIMILATIVE

INSTINCTIVE
	Abalone
	Amianth
	Leopardskin Agate
	Blue Aventurine
	Benjaninite
	BONE
	Black Coral
	Apple Coral
	Flint
|Gray/Black Grossular|
	IVORY
	Brown or Gray Jade
	Morrison Ranch
	Jasper
	Lawsonite
	Ludlamite
	Cameo Shell
	Mother of Pearl Shell
	Black Obsidian
	Petrified Wood
	Scheelite

CENTER COMBINATIONS:

Aragonite	Benitoite
Black Jade	Green Aventurine
Blue Calcite	Smithsonite
Red Aventurine	Galena

53

CHIEF FEATURES

CHIEF FEATURES: "A primary stumbling block we
have set up so we can learn about the
characteristics and consequences of that
particular fear."(2)

SELF-DEPRECATION: Self worth is felt to be very
low. The fear is "of being inadequate."(2)

CARNELIAN: Softens self-deprecation and arrogance,
particularly self-deprecation. Allows one to temporarily put
aside major self esteem issues and questions such as "What
am I really worth?" Major questions like this as well as others
such as "I'm so embarrassed to be seen in public with my new
hairdo" feel laid to rest --not that they're handled or will never
come up again. Thus, one gets a break from needing to be
better than anyone else or agonizing over how inferior to
others one feels. This creates the space for some positive
feedback to flow in. Also balancing for high frequency,
mid-range male/female energy types.

CHALCOPYRITE: For self-esteem. The energy of this stone
keeps you feeling good about yourself and seeing yourself
in a positive light. Makes you feel you are worthwhile, useful
worth member of society. Most stones that relate to chief
features, just help you notice what you're doing. This stone
actually changes how you feel about yourself.

CHROMITE: Softens self-deprecation. Makes you notice how
self-deprecating you're being and it becomes too
embarrassing to continue. Especially since it usually is found
with Kammererite which connects one with the Buddhaic
plane. Hard to maintain belief that one is worse than
everything and everyone else when one is part of it all.

SPESSARTITE: Softens self-deprecation and arrogance.
The "homemaker" stone. Makes one feel contented and
happy with one's home life. Brings up feelings such as "I'm
a good person. I have my niche. I know where I belong and
that's in the home and with my family. I feel grounded; I feel
rooted. So, it's unnecessary for me to self-deprecate or be
arrogant.

PEACH SPINEL: Softens self-deprecation and arrogance.
Hits you very hard with the realization that you just did or said

54

something self-deprecating or arrogant.

YELLOW SPINEL: Softens arrogance and self-deprecation. Pushes away the self-deprecation and pulls one into the positive pole of arrogance and a feeling of pride. I can take this one circumstance and I can say I have a right to be proud of that. I can increase my self-esteem. Particularly good for people who are extremely self-deprecating.

ARROGANCE: **Low self esteem is covered by a facade of 'I' m O.K. or an air of superiority. The fear is of "being judged and found wanting, i.e., vulnerability."(2)**

AMBLYGONITE: Reduces arrogance by taking the attention off the self. Directs the attention outward to noticing other people, the surroundings and the point of the situation in which you find yourself. Different colors better for certain types.

GOLD: Solid types; i.e. a person who's very grounded and organized.

PINK: Fluid types; i.e., a person who's more flowing, expansive, and fluffy.

CLEAR: Good for all.

EMERALDS: Softens arrogance. Brings up question "Am I thinking I am better than anyone else. Should I be watching that? I know I'm privileged, or rich or good-looking or whatever, but am I using it to make me think I'm better than somebody else?" Exalted roles are particularly prone to this. Also balancing for high frequency, mid-range male/female energy types. Enhances communication and is also referred to as a sage stone.

GOUDIMITE: Decreases arrogance. Keeps one from having "shy episodes:" i.e., that agonizing flipping back and forth between self-deprecation and arrogance. This stone short circuits the process. Good for children since they usually go through this.

SPESSARTITE: See self-deprecation.

PEACH SPINEL: See self-deprecation.

YELLOW SPINEL: See self-deprecation.

SELF-DESTRUCTION: The "act or motivation to harm oneself either physically or emotionally."(2) The fear is that life will never be worth living.

AMAZONITE: (Green Microcline). Softens self-destruction. Gives you the feeling you can have what you want and that you don't have to do self-destructive things. It makes you see just how self-destructive you are when you're taking that drink or engaging in some other bad habit. You really feel just how unnecessary it is. Pulls one into the positive pole of greed and that one can get out there and get the things or experiences one wants.

MICROCLINE: (White and pink). Very anti self-destruction. Makes it difficult to operate in a way that is harmful to the self.

GREED: "The experience of wanting, or desiring, out of a fear there will not be enough to go around."(2)

BLOODSTONE: (Some forms called Heliotrope). Softens greed. Pulls one into the positive pole of greed. Engenders a strong feeling that it is all right to have what you want and that it is only a matter of time until you get it. High prosperity consciousness and willingness for abundance to show up in one's life. One feels confident that life will be good and thus, self esteem is raised.

NUNKIRCHNER JASPER: (Sometimes called Hornstone). Same in effect as Bloodstone.

MARTYRDOM: The feeling that one is a victim of the circumstances and that those circumstances are beyond one's control. The fear is "that their only value lies in being a victim."(2)

BOWENITE: (Also called New Jade or China Jade). Anti-martyrdom stone. Eases one's sense of being victimized by others or by one's circumstances. Useful for those in impatience or stubbornness who slide to martyrdom once in a while. Also good to give to anyone in the generation that went through the depression since most have a sense of martyrdom they've never been able to shake. One reason Bowenite helps one feel less of a victim is that it balances the hormonal system as well. See Sexuality.

CRYSTAL with a Blue Tinge: (Occurs naturally). Curbs impatience and martyrdom.

ERYTHRITE: Softens martyrdom. Pulls one into the positive pole of martyrdom; selflessness. Good for those who have a tendency to be too self centered and thinking too much of just themselves.

IMPATIENCE: **Impatience often feels there is not enough time and operates from a fear "of missing out."(2) Intolerance at its worst and audacity at its best characterizes impatience.**

AMETHYST: Softens impatience and martyrdom. Extremely popular since most people feel either impatient or victimized at one time or another in their lives. Particularly effective for impatience. The more transparent and dark purple the color, the more intense the effect. Balancing and grounding for high frequency types. Balances extreme male/female energy.

ROYAL BLUE CRYSTAL: (Man-made and color added). Softens impatience.

DANBURITE: Curbs impatience. Particularly good for the very heavily impatient: i.e., For those who can be extremely intolerant; for the type of person who will hyperventilate if caught in a traffic jam because they can't stand the slow pace.

STUBBORNESS: **Operates with a great deal of determination and purpose and can become obstinate even when this is not in their best interest. The fear is of "losing one's personal integrity."(2)**

BLUE, WHITE & LAVENDER LACE AGATE: Softens stubbornness.

AZURITE: Softens stubbornness but very mild in its action. Azurite allows you to be in better communication and since communication involves a willingness to listen, one has to be less stubborn in the sense that one is off one's position. Assists communication generally. Also balances low frequency, mid-range male/female energy types.

GOLDEN TIGER EYE: Softens stubbornness. Works in an unusual fashion. Pulls one into the positive pole of their attitude and makes it possible to be determined rather than obstinate.   Does this only for those whose chief feature is stubbornness. Balancing for low frequency types. Very attractive to more solid types who like to move slowly and take their time about things.

ALL-PURPOSE: **There are several minerals that erase all chief features and pull you into the positive pole of your attitude.** They are:
BRECCHIATED AGATE: (Also called Canal Agate and Tubular Agate).
RIM JASPER: (Also called Wood Jasper).

CHIEF FEATURES

The term "chief feature" is short for chief negative feature. So, all the qualities listed below are not those we desire to cultivate. The gemstones work in two ways: 1) a gemstone will pull you into the positive pole of the specific feature and 2) a gemstone softens a chief feature by making you aware that you are doing it (e.g., being impatient) and thus, it is a little harder to keep on doing it.

	ORDINAL	EXALTED
INSPIRATION	**SELF DEP** |CARNELIAN |Chalcopyrite |Chromite |Spessartite |Peach Spinel |Yellow Spinel	**ARROGANCE** |Ambllygonite |EMERALDS |Goudimite |Spessatite |PEACH SPINEL |Yellow Spinel
EXPRESSION	**SELF DESTRUCT** |AMAZONITE |Microcline |	**GREED** |AMAZONITE |Bloodstone |Nunkirchner Jasp
ACTION	**MARTYRDOM** |AMETHYST |Bowenite |Erythrite	**IMPATIENCE** |AMETHYST |Royal Blu Crystal |Danburite

NEUTRAL

ASSIMILATIVE	**STUBBORNESS** |BLUE LACE AGATE | |White Lace Agate | |Lavendar Lace Agat | |Azurite | |Golden Tiger Eye |

ALL-PURPOSE: (These erase all chief features).
BRECCHIATED AGATE, RIM JASPER, and WOOD JASPER.

COMMUNICATION

These stones open up your willingness to listen to other persons and communicate with them as well as their willingness to listen to you. Communication is extremely important. It is not possible for sentient beings to evolve without communication because all evolution occurs in relationship to other sentient beings. The primary distinction between sentient beings and non-sentient beings, besides the awareness that "I am I," is the fact that sentient beings talk about things. If we stop talking about things we really take a step backwards down the evolutionary scale. Communication need not be verbal, but it is necessary that, by some means, what is going on with one's self is communicated to others and similar communications received.

ANTLERITE: Pulls one strongly into good, clear communication and, thus, eliminates arguing. Makes it difficult, if not impossible, to miscommunicate.

ARDENNITE: For sociability, communication ,and adaptability especially if one has a tendency to be a wallflower. Promotes stage I type of communication which is "I need to say something non-threatening here to get an interaction started so we can get to know each other. " Helps one start to make friends.

AZURITE: Assists communication generally. Makes one clearer in communication, i.e., able to get one's point across more clearly. See Chief Features and Frequency.

CHESSYLITE: Same in effect as Azurite.

BISMUTH: A "Storyteller" stone. Aids imagination and storytelling ability.

GREEN CRYSTAL: Predisposes one to talking and disseminating information.

EMERALDS: Keep you balanced, in communication, and away from arrogant or self-deprecating communication. See roles and chief features.

GREEN GROSSULAR: Basically makes you more comfortable with communicating; i.e., feel more comfortable with what you want to say and your ability to communicate it.

KORNERUPINE: (Grass green, pine green, or green-brown). Enables one to communicate more clearly. The greener the color, the stronger the effect.

LODESTONE: Helps one communicate with dolphins and whales who are sentient beings.

MALACHITE: Makes you feel very grounded and balanced and very willing to communicate who you are and where you're coming from. Very willing to relate to others and let them know what your position is.

MYRICHITE: For accuracy and speed of communication. Communication is more intense in quality and one feels a strong push to get one's communications out there quickly. Good for those in the media and for others who just need to have an "important" talk with someone.

SAGENITE AGATE: (Purple agate with threads of white). Use to be more direct and clear in your expression. The white crystals provide power energy which makes communications more purposeful and powerful. It contains Purple Lace Agate which softens stubbornness and makes you more willing to share. Anyone will find this stone useful, but it is particularly balancing for the expressive roles (sages and artisans) since that is what they are all about.

PURPLE SPINEL: Good for communicating with people who are very different in age from oneself either older or younger. A generation gap stone. See Roles.

YELLOW SPINEL: Encourages communication from the standpoint of a feeling of pride in oneself. "I am proud of myself and I want to tell you about it." See chief features.

GREEN SPINEL: A wisdom stone. Assists in communication of wisdom. This only works, of course, if you have something wise to say. See Roles.

TEKTITE: (From meteors). The "UFO" stone. Assists in contacting and communicating with sentient beings from other planets.

GREEN TOURMALINE: Produces a sagelike ability to communciate.

UVARIVITE: A "Storyteller" stone. Aids imagination and storytelling ability.

GREEN ZIRCON: Increases gregariousness. Similar in effect to Ardennite.

CHANNELING

Channeling is bringing in energy other than your own from the universe connecting you either with someone from a higher plane of existence, a "consciousness," or with a bit of energy from a higher plane of existence. This then translates into intellectual information you can use, an emotional impact you can use, or healing energy you can use. Another way to express this is that channeling means to bring someone in who does not have a body, at the present time, so that they can have a mouth.

Channeling one's own essence is not really channeling. This just means you are in touch with your essence. Channeling spirit guides means you're in touch with entities astrally who are working with you deliberately to move you forward because they're buddies of yours and want to help you out. You can bring them in and talk with them in your head or leave and let them use your body to talk with someone else.

Rocks are an aid in channeling in that they soften or remove blocks to channeling. In trying out the various stones, you can find the one that works for you and, thus, pinpoint what your block was. Some people have difficulty channeling in from a specific source. Instead, they will have energy flooding in from everywhere. You can use a rock that connects you with a specific plane to fine tune or focus into that specific source.

Some stones work better depending on what your frequency is. A high frequency person might prefer a high energy stone such as Sugilite. A lower frequency person might prefer the Aventurines as the gentler energy might feel less intrusive. It is very important to keep chakras open, aligned, and balanced so energy can flow through unimpeded. This enables one to channel for a longer period of time without feeling exhausted later.

Opening the chakras:
BLUE AVENTURINE: Opens and unblocks the first chakra.*
GREEN AVENTURINE: Opens and unblocks the sixth and
   seventh chakra.*
RED AVENTURINE: Opens and unblocks the second through
   fifth chakras.*
BLUE CALCITE: Opens, heals and unblocks all chakras.*

COBALT GLASS; BLUE, ORANGE & RED: Opens the
    seventh chakra.
CHALCANTHITE: (Poisonous Copper Sulfate). Opens the
    seventh chakra and the higher emotional center. The effect
    is very strong and it is important to be grounded and have all
    chakras aligned and balanced before using this stone to
    channel. Helpful to those who are super intellectual or
    moving centered and have difficulty getting into the
    emotional center; it would open them up to higher
    emotionally centered experiences and a feeling they could
    love all mankind.
GRANITE: To connect one with the Tao; opens the seventh
    chakra.
SUGILITE: Very powerful channeling stone, opens up all
    chakras to higher influences particularly the seventh.

Aligning and balancing chakras:
ARAGONITE: Keeps chakras four, five, and six in open, in
    balance and aligned.*
BENITOITE: Healing to the chakras.*
COBALT: (An orchid colored rock in a brown matrix). This
    stone has the effect of a combination of Sugilite and
    Clevelandite. Very useful for opening up one's channeling
    abilities. When heat treated, cobalt becomes cobalt glass
    (see above) and is much milder in effect.
CLEVELANDITE: Channeling aid. Balances and grounds
    while channeling. Keeps chakras   automatically aligned and
    healed. Enables a person to channel twice as long without
    getting   tired.
BLACK JADE: Balances the lower three chakras.*
SEPTARIAN NODULE: Composed of Concretions, Aragonite
    and Brown Calcite. Most useful if one is already a channel.
    The concretions contain Divac energy and can also provide a
    base for your astral guides to connect with you from. This
    lends you a great deal of energy, support, and power during
    the channeling process. The Aragonite keeps chakras four,
    five and six open, in balance and aligned. And the Brown
    Calcite allows you to connect with the Mental Plane which is a
    source of informational energy and higher truth.
SCHEELITE: Balances the first chakra.

Selecting the source:
APACHE TEARS: Assists in communication with one's
    essence and particularly good for channeling in one's spirit

63

guides. Enables one to get in touch with those entities who care about you and want to communicate with you.

APOPHYLLITE (ANGEL STONE): Connects one with the cycled-off members of one's entity.

BERRYLIUM: Connects one with the Messianic Plane.

WHITE CALCITE: (ICELAND SPAR). Connects one with the Messianic Plane.*

BROWN or GOLD CALCITE: Connects one with the Mental Plane and higher information.*

HIDDENITE: (Green SPODUMENE). Connects one with the Messianic Plane or Buddhaic Plane.

KAMMERERITE: Connects one with the Buddhaic Plane.*

KYANITE: Connects one to the Causal Plane and Michael.*

LEPIDOLITE: Connects one with the Buddhaic Plane

MUSCOVITE: Connects one with spirit guides and the Astral Plane. Similar to Apache Tears. Assists solid types in leaving their bodies.

ROSE QUARTZ: Assists one in communicating with one's essence and spirit guides. Since Rose Quartz keeps you in your body, the communication would take place internally.

SHATTUCKITE: Puts you in touch with different degrees of essence: i.e., from the least to the most developed parts of your essence.

STELLARITE: Puts you in touch with the highest degree of your essence.

*For more information, see the section on Centers.

SHAMANISM

ENARGITE: A shaman stone. Discovered centuries ago and used by shamans for vision quests and in combination with drugs for heavy hallucinatory experiences. Tends to put you more in alignment with your astral self than your physical self. In general, promotes vivid dreaming, so it can be used by those who wish to remember their dreams more.

HAUYNITE: Amplifies shamanic abilities. Puts you in the emotional center and really in touch with those infant lifetimes when you were still in touch with the Tao. Feel Buddhaic connectedness and able to use symbolism to reach higher states. It is an ingredient in Lapis Lazuli.

MORRISON RANCH JASPER: Same in effect as Morrisonite. Pus you in touch with the Tao in a shamanistic way. Makes it easier to get in touch with inner parts of the self using rituals and ritualistic symbology. Also useful in doing instinctive regression work or in accepting certain types of change in one's life.

MORRISONITE: Related to Shamanistic type rituals. Makes it possible to get more out of the ritual; feel the energy more closely and connectedly the way infant souls and old souls do as they are more connected to the Tao. Opens the connection through all chakras. The more the avocado green color is included, the more effective it is because that's where the energy is stored.

BALANCE, ENERGY & FREQUENCY

Michael highly recommends putting the focus on being in balance and regards the stones for balancing to be among the most important. To be in balance means the chakras are aligned and that energy can flow through them freely: that energy, as it moves through the body, doesn't run into blocks and one doesn't feel unconscious or stuck. A key to dealing with stress is to come into life or into any situation from being in balance. Then whatever happens is not nearly as stressful as those same things occurring when one is not in balance or harmony with oneself. Most of us do it the other way around. We get all "stressed out" and then look for some way to lower or handle the stress. If you look in the mental and emotional stress section, you will find a number of stones that help you deal with stress once it has been created.

"Frequency" refers to the rate at which one's internal clock runs. For those of higher frequency, the internal clock runs faster and they want to zip through life. A person of lower frequency tends to have a denser body and move more slowly through life. Each person has a natural set point with regard to frequency, but it is possible to consciously raise or lower one's frequency. The stones are an aid in this regard. A stone that is listed as balancing to a high frequency person will raise the frequency of a low frequency person. A stone that is listed as balancing a low frequency person will lower the frequency of a high frequency person. There is also a group of stones that enable you to match frequencies with other persons.

The use of the word energy can refer to the amount of juice one has in one's batteries. There are a number of stones that are energizing and a number of stones that drain out excess energy and help you relax. Energy can also be divided into two types: male energy which is the focused, organized, and very grounded approach to life and female energy which is unfocused, creative, and expansive approach to life. Each person has a certain proportion of male energy to female energy that is not dependent on gender. Thus a woman can be very high male energied or high female energied or just about 50/50, as can men.

BALANCE: All the stones listed below are for balancing. They are also organized according to how they affect persons of different frequency. If you don't know your frequency or can't guess, just pick the ones you like.

Low (1 - 30%) or High (70 - l00%) male or female energy:
  High Frequency: Moss, Fern, Tree or Dendrite Agate, Amethyst, Clam Shell Snow Flake Obsidian, and Tanzanite
  Low Frequency: Apache Tears, Green Aventurine Bloodstone, Green Jasper, Tiger eye and Nunkirchner Jasper

Mid-range (31 - 69%) male or female energy:
  High Frequency: Emeralds, Carnelian, Moss, Fern, Tree or Dendritic Agates, and Snow Flake Obsidian
  Low Frequency: Apache Tears, Tlger Eye (Blue or Gold), Azurite, and Chessylite

FELDSPAR: For integrating, grounding and balancing. Each type is role related.
  ALBITE: (Blue, clear & white). Mature and old priests.
  ANDESINE: Mature and old artisans.
  ANORTHITE: Mature and old scholars.
  BYTOWNITE: Mature and old kings.
  LABRADORITE: Mature and old warriors.
  OLIGOCLASE: Mature and old sages.
  RED to BROWN: Mature and old servers.
MALACHITE: Most powerful balancing stone. Balancing for everyone, but especially those in the 50-50 male/female energy range.
BRICK-RED JASPER: All purpose balancer.

FREQUENCY:

It is the primary function of the metals to raise or lower frequency. Remember, when one's frequency is raised, one feels zippier and when one's frequency is lowered one feels more mellow.

GOLD: Lowers frequency the most.

BRONZE and BRASS: Lowers frequency, but not quite as much as gold.

COPPER: Raises frequency most powerfully and is, thus, quite energizing.

SILVER: Raises frequency a moderate amount.

MATCHING ENERGIES:

APACHE GOLD: Same in effect as Iron Pyrite.

ARSENAPYRITE: Helps you match energies (male/female) with someone of different balance than yourself.

COPCO AGATE: (Carnelian with a thin layer of White Agate on top). Balances a high frequency person or helps a lower frequency person raise their frequency. A very balancing and healing energy surrounded with the loving emotionality of the Venusian body-type Agate.

LIMONITE: Same in effect as Iron Pyrite.

IRON PYRITE: Helps one match frequency with someone of a higher or lower frequency than yourself.

PYRRHOTITE: Same in effect as Iron Pyrite.

MALE/FEMALE ENERGY:

GREEN CHLORITE: Attractive to those with female bodies or high female energy. Creates comfort and compatibility for a high male-energied person in a female body or a high female-energied person in a male body. Often found with Quartz which adds an element of observation and clarity to the adjustment process.

COLEMANITE: (Looks like Mesolite). A female energy rock that enhances female energy and unfocus. Useful for someone who has too much male energy and wants to learn to use or experience their female energy more.

COVELLITE: Increases male energy (focused energy) by putting you in touch with the male energy you have. Enables you to use your male energy more cleverly and quickly regardless of the amount of male energy you have.

67

GOETHITE: Similar to Chlorite, but attractive to those with male bodies or high male energy. Makes high female energy types more comfortable with a masculine body, and high male energy types more comfortable with a female body. Because this stone reduces the amount of conflict going on internally, one feels much more relaxed. Also good for men having a hard time with masculinity issues such as feeling they're not masculine enough or not in touch with their male side. Found in Flourite or Quartz Crystals.

GREEN JASPER: Balances and heals extreme male energied and low frequency types.

GYROLITE: Accentuates the qualities of female energy: e.g., unfocusedness, ability to look in many directions at once and creativity. Puts you more in touch with your female energy and your ability to use it.

IMPERIAL JASPER: (Purplish/red). For someone who's very unfocused and wants to get focused; for a high female-energied person who wants to get grounded. Conversely, also useful for someone of a very low frequency to feel healed because they're always striving to be higher. Has two different sides to what it does.

MARBLE: Balances the male energied side of everyone. Makes it easier to accomplish projects that require a high degree of focus and concentration. Darker colors are preferred by those with a high percentage of male energy or by the more solid roles such as warriors, kings and scholars. Lighter colors of marble are preferred by high female energy types, by the lighter roles and by those who feel very unhealed and sensitive.

OKENITE: Balances high female energied types and promotes creativity. Very useful as it is easy for those with high female energy to get out of balance.

ONYX: Balances the female energied side of everyone. Useful when one wants to pursue creative projects and see things from a more expansive, "larger picture" perspective. Darker colors are more intense and preferred by high male energied types or by the more solid roles. Correspondingly, lighter colors are gentler and usually preferred by the high female energied types. Similar to Marble in this aspect.

WATERMELON TOURMALINE: Helps very fluid types manifest their solidity and very female energied types manifest their male energy.

HEALING and HEALTH MAINTENANCE

The most important thing to understand is that all gemstones and minerals are 'healing' in the sense they have a positive effect on one's physical, emotional and/or intellectual functioning. The use of the term 'healing' in this pamphlet specifically indicates that a malfunction of some kind exists in the body and needs correction. Healing occurs because a stone focuses a healing energy on the body that vibrates at a particular frequency. Healing will generally be successful unless, for self-karmic reasons, the individual does not wish to be healed.

A word about crystals are in order since they have a very strong reputation as healers. There are other minerals that are stronger healers such as Variegated Jasper. In general, all Jaspers and Agates are very healing. They are the same chemical composition and differ in name only. Crystals (rock crystals) heal by clearing the area of the body they are placed near. Thus, if a chakra is blocked, a crystal will clear it; if one is congested, a crystal will clear up the congestion. In addition, crystals have the special quality of being very individual. Each crystal has a slightly different character and heals in a slightly different way. Any particular person will resonate to one and not to another. Leaded crystal (man-made crystal) does not have the same individuality or power although it still produces clarity.

THE PHYSICAL BODY:
GENERAL:
BRAZILIAN AGATE: Healing to the kidneys.
MOSS & FERN : Healing in general.
ANDRADITE; DEMANTOID: (Emerald Green) Heals veins.
              MELANITE: (Black) Heals skin.
              TOPAZOLITE: (Yellow) Heals synapses.
ANGLESITE: Healing for hardening of the arteries.
BRACHANTITE: Heals the lungs, esophagus, and throat. Also heals cancer in those areas.
CYANOTRICHITE: Balances hormones. Stimulates hair growth. The balancing and stimulating of the hormones engages the emotions. This has the effect of creating an emotional intensity and depth that is psychologically transformational.
CHRYSOBERYL: Found mostly in these colors in the locations particular to each race.

69

CAT'S EYE: General healing for Asians and South Americans.

GOLDEN: General healing for Australians.

YELLOW-GREEN: General healing for Europeans and North Americans.

BROWN: General healing for Africans.

LAVENDAR to PURPLE CRYSTAL: Balancing physically.

DESCLOIZITE: Removes external aberrant growths such as warts, moles, skin growths, blisters and hives.

DIOPSIDE: For fever. Balances body temperature or reduces aches due to an imbalance in temperature.

DOLOMITE: Promotes general internal bodily health.

GORDONITE: Healing to the myelin sheath; the outer covering of muscle cells.

WHITE GROSSULAR: Healing to the immune system.

PINK JASPER: Hormone balancing.

VARIEGATED JASPER: Strongest healing stone. Especially for those who have been extremely ill and are recuperating. Anything that was shattering or extremely debilitating to the body can be handled by this stone.

YELLOW JASPER: Hormone balancing.

NORTHRUPITE: Increases muscle strength.

LEUCITE: (Clear or white). Helps clear mucus membranes. Good for colds.

LIMESTONE: Extremely healing to the immune system; keeps it in order.

ORTHOCLASE: Anti-cancer agent.

PYROPHYLLITE: Heals and detoxifies the blood.

SANIDINE: (A variety of Orthoclase). Anti-cancer agent.

VIOLANE: Balances body temperature and reduces fever.

RED ZIRCON: Helps ear infections heal more quickly.

ALLERGIES:

POPPY JASPER: For animal allergies. Keeps you from being allergic to the animals or to their products: e.g., feathers in pillows, horsehair or any part one might eat such as meat. Also helps one to understand animals and get more in tune with them. Creates more compatibility with one's pets.

GOLD BERYL: Heals allergies to plants and pollens.

WHITE BERYL: Heals dust allergies.

GREEN CALCITE: Heals allergies to toxic fumes and chemicals.

SERPENTINE: (Chartreuse in color). Reduces allergic

reactions to animals, birds, fish, reptiles, pets and meats to eat.
SULFUR: Heals plant allergies.

BONES:
BOLIVARITE: Healing for the joints of the body.
CELENITE ROSE: To keep calcium in your bones; especially
   good for women.
DOLOMITE: Kills off aberrant cells and promotes correct bone
   growth. Very mild in its action.
HOPEITE: For healing bone marrow.
WAVELLITE: Healing for bones:
   BLUE: Small bones
   BROWN: Teeth.
   COLORLESS: Larger bones.
   GREEN: Medium-size bones.
   WHITE & YELLOW: Bone marrow.

CLEANSING AND PURIFYING:
GREEN CALCITE: Clears toxins from the body and the
   atmosphere:
LIMESTONE: Totally cleansing and purifying to the system.
   Strong grounding rock.
PYROPHYLLITE: Heals and detoxifies the blood.
TACHIANTITE: (DO NOT INGEST!) Aids the body's cleansing,
   flushing and elimination of any excesses: e.g., excess
   bacteria and viruses, excess toxins, excess water, excess fat.
   Good for losing weight.

FOOD and DIGESTION:
DOLOMITE: Aids in digestion.
EUDIALYTE: Related to vitamin absorption, particularly those
   that are fatty based or occur in complex or yang foods, e.g.,
   nuts, fish, meats
LONG-HAIR ASBESTOS: Aids digestion when worn on the
   body close to the esophogas or stomach. Also good for
   eating unfamiliar foods as when traveling in a foreign country
   or eating unusual amounts of food. It basically reduces
   stomach acid production and allows the body to digest food
   better.
PIOCHE: Heals the digestive tract.
PROUSTITE: Heals the colon.
LT. BROWN SARD: Aids in digesting vegetable proteins.
RED BROWN SARD: Aids in digesting animal proteins.
SELENITE: Aids in the digestion and absorption of minerals.

71

SERPENTINE: (Chartreuse in color). Reduces allergy to eating meats.

FUNGUS:
BARITE: Fungus removal
CERUSSITE: Fungus removal.

PAIN:
CROCOITE: Heals back and headache pain.
LATTICE AGATE: Eliminates Headaches.
BROWN ZIRCON: Heals headaches. Drains excess energy from head and keeps energy appropriate in that part of the body.

HEALING for VARIOUS FREQUENCIES:
HIGH FREQUENCY: Abalone and Clam Shell. (See instinctive center).
LOW FREQUENCY: Green Jasper and Imperial Jasper. (See balance, energy & frequency).

SEXUALITY: (Also see Higher Kinesthetic Center)
WONDER AGATE: For male sexuality. Increases sexual arousal and the ability to get and maintain erections.
BARTHITE: Makes one feel more comfortable with one's sexual idiosyncrasies. An idiosyncrasy is defined here as a normal sexual behavior that is unacceptable to the culture; e.g., homosexuality, bisexuality, etc. A healing rock that would go well with Zebra Agate.
SPONGE CORAL: Recreational and non-karmic sex of the "let's have fun" variety. Not very intense but fun. Associated with a more childlike and innocent view of sex without too much stuff about it. Can also enjoy flirtations. Moving part of the sexual center.
CHLOROMELANITE: (Black jade and bright green jadeite mixed together). Very balancing for women in the area of sexual identity. Gives a woman a clear sense of who she is as a woman; enables her to be comfortable and grounded in her femininity.
YELLOW JADE: (Usually is a cream color). Takes the mystery out of the opposite sex and gives you a sense you really can understand what goes on with them. Intellectual part of the sexual center.
BRICK-RED JASPER: Helps one get along with the same sex.

72

If homosexual, makes one very comfortable with their
sexuality and helps one maintain compatible same-sex
relationships. Also functions as a general balancing stone.
Found in great quantities in California.

SERAPE JASPER: For female sexuality. Stimulates sexual
arousal and facilitates getting pregnant.

WILLOW CREEK JASPER: Same in effect as Serape Jasper.

NATROJAROSITE: Reduces sexual repression and increases
passion by lifting the lid off the repression.

MAHOGANY OBSIDIAN: Increases one's sexuality and
sensuality. One feels sexier and more "in touch with touch."

RYALITE: A generic name for Serape Jasper and Wonder
Agate. The more pink/orange the tones are, the more the
stone relates to female sexuality. The more
brown/gray/purple the tones are, the more the stone relates
to male sexuality.

SUNSTONE: In general, a second chakra stone relating to
sexuality. Each color has a slilghtly different effect.

ORANGE or PINK: For finding sexual relationships. Gives the
wearer an aura of sexual attractiveness.

CLEAR or YELLOW: For maintaining sexual relationships and
keeping them balanced. All couples could use this. Helps
avoid the tendency to blame the partner for difficulties.

BLUE or GREEN: For ending sexual relationships
appropriately.

REPRODUCTION:

BUORNONITE: Increases hereditary red-headedness in
children of those who wear it.

BOWENITE: (Also called New Jade, Serpentine or Transvaal
Jade). Healing and balancing to the female reproductive
system and organs. Good if pregnant: keeps mother and
fetus in alignment. Keeps everything related to the
pregnancy functioning normally and in good shape.
Reduces risk of birth defects and protects growth of children
particularly female children. Also anti-martyrdom stone. See
chief features.

CONACHALCITE: To put mother and fetus in balance with
each other.

CORNETITE: Increases fertility. Promotes sperm production;
stimulates healthy functioning of reproductive organs.

CUPRITE: Birth control rock. Aids in avoiding conception and
increases the chances for abortion by making it difficult for

73

the fetus to attach itself to the uterine wall. (Poisonous. Don't eat it!).

DIABASE: For fertility and potency. Makes it easier to "get" pregnant or "make" someone pregnant. Steps up sperm production, beneficial influence on health of sex organs and helps maintain erections.

LIBETHENITE: This stone is good to keep around when one is trying to get pregnant. It kills off aberrant sex cells, especially aberrant sperm cells. Thus, it lowers the risk of a baby that's mentally retarded or deformed.

PETALITE: (Clear or pink). Aids in fertility. Promotes sperm production; acts on the sexual organs to stimulate healthy functioning.

WEIGHT CONTROL: (Also see section of Eliminating Bad Habits for control of compulsions, and the sections on the Kinesthetic Center and Energizing for encouraging one to exercise).

INESITE: Balances water gain and loss in the body.

LANARKITE: (White-lavendar crystals). Helps you lose weight. Boosts the metabolic rate.

TACCHANTITE: (DO NOT INGEST). Aids the body in cleansing, flushing and eliminating any exesses: e.g., excess water and fat. Good for losing weight.

TENNANTITE: Helps you gain weight. Slows down the metabolic rate.

MENTAL STRESS:

BRECCHIATED JASPER: Heals mental stress. Centers you intellectually and makes it easier to be logical, clear headed and clear thinking. Wakes you up and increases your intellectual capacity.

DIOPTASE: Healing for the brain. This refers to anything that physically stresses the brain: e.g., edema, a mild concussion and stress chemicals released into the brain from overstudying, or overworking.

OPALITE: Pulls excess energy in the body up and out. Particularly useful for those who tend to stay in their heads and overuse the intellectual centers.

EMOTIONAL STRESS:

STRESS REDUCTION: (Also see Emotional and Instinctive Centers)

LEOPARD SKIN AGATE: Very grounding and healing when dealing with heavy emotional issues. Reduces free-floating anxiety; i.e., when you're worried and anxious, but don't know why. Grounding for people who are paranoid or schizophrenic and those who are totally unstable and cannot handle life.

A stone used for centuries. Called Wolfstone at one time because unconsciously it was recognized that the wolf is directly related to, and the symbol for, the emotional part of the instinctive center. Thus, this stone puts you in touch with any instinctive terrors or fears so you can work on them and conquer them.

AURICHALCITE: For stress-related emotional healing. Particularly useful when one has taken some real hard knocks emotionally and the emotional center (heart chakra) needs healing.

EDINGTONITE: Softens grief; i.e., if in heavy grief, softens it and allows you to get through it without collapse.

KINOITE: Promotes a feeling of peace and harmony. Aids in the easing of grief.

LAWSONITE: Very grounding and healing when dealing with heavy emotional issues. Same in effect as Leopard Skin Agate.

PAUA SHELL: Helpful in difficult karmas or or soul-level transitions. Heals stress by keeping body clear of stressful body chemicals and hormones.

CALMING:

ANALCITE QUARTZ: (Clear like crystal, but occurs in squares instead of points). Has a very stable, cleansing, and anchoring energy. Works like a quadrant; very stable and secure. Enables one to handle anything that comes up with a sense of purpose and ability to remain neutral.

CRYSTAL, LT. GREEN: (Leaded crystal). Calming.

BLUE GOLDSTONE: (Glass with copper flecks. The blue color is a dye). Copper raises one's frequency or "buzziness," but is somewhat softened by the glass which surrounds it. The dark blue color is very calming particularly if intellectually stressed. The total effect is one of making you feel you can enjoy your time off or a feel a little peppier if tired.

LAVENDER QUARTZ: (Also called Cape Amethyst). Calming. Relieves Stress. Aids meditation and self remembering. Self-remembering is being aware of what one is actually doing and saying on all levels. An intense, supra-self awareness.

NEPHRITE: (Green Jade). Produces tranquility. Good for depression. (See Attitudes).

PREHNITE: Promotes calm.

PINK with BROWN or YELLOW or GREY RHODONITE: For maintaining one's dignity and "cool" during trying circumstances.

SPIDER-WEB JASPER: Soothes frayed nerves. Valium-like in effect.

CONQUERING FEARS: (Also see instinctive center)

CELESTITE: Related to high altitudes. Enables one to adjust to a higher altitude (thinner air) more quickly, particularly if you move from sea level to someplace high. Thus, useful for skiing and mountain vacations. Good for air travel phobia or fear of heights in general. Helps adjust to higher altitudes with less fear and less motion sickness.

EMERADA: (Lt. Green Spinel) For fearlessness: feel less fear.

HALOTRICHITE: Calms fear of heights. Works like Celestite except that one has a sense of transcending into spiritual heights as well as physical heights. Halotrichite is also more related to fears about heights stemming from traumatic incidents in past lives that one is still afraid of now.

HYPERSTHENE: (Clear black-green or black-brown). Helps reduce fear about being in public view. For example, useful in public speaking, board meetings, or crowded grocery stores.

MOLYBDENITE: To feel comfortable in the dark.

RAMSDELLITE: Increases courage. Gives you the courage to continue in very difficult, dangerous or potentially dangerous situations. Helps you operate from "fight" rather than "flight."

STIBNITE: Enables one to feel more brave.

ELIMINATING BAD HABITS:

BLACK and BROWN OBSIDIAN: (Also called Golden Obsidian). Helps eliminate bad habits by reducing craving. Good for dieting, giving up smoking and other bad habits.

PHENACITE: COLORLESS: Prevents one from forming bad
mental habits.
YELLOW-PINK: Prevents one from forming bad
physical habits.
CAMEO SHELL: Good for eliminating bad habits. Opens the
instinctive center and allows one to look at whether they
need to keep the habit around any more. Allows evaluation
of the usefulness of any particular habit.
WITHERITE: Helps control compulsions. Compulsions stem
from being trapped in the emotional part of the moving
center. One acts without thinking, then feels negatively
about one's action. This is followed again by the same action
and then negative emotion and then the same action and so
on. This stone brea s the cycle by allowing one to move into
another center such as the intellectual center where one can
think about what one is doing or into a different type of action
which might be more appropriate or pleasing to the
individual.

WELL BEING:
HAPPINESS:
FLAME AGATE: Same in effect as Zebra Agate.
ZEBRA AGATE: For adjusting to and being comfortable in your
body. For enjoying your body and the activities you do in it.
AJOITE: Puts you in a good mood. Enables you to see the
lighter side of things.
AUTINITE: (Brown/green or yellow). Makes you feel more
adventurous: like trying out some new places, people or
things and having a little fun.
CRYSTAL, ORANGE, TAN & CHAMPAGNE: (Leaded crystal).
Feel happier and more balanced.
CRYSTAL, RASPBERY: (Leaded crystal). Makes one feel
exuberant and festive; ready to party.
FANCY JASPER: "Let's party" stone. (Dark green shading to
violet.) To lighten up those who are extremely male
energied. Helps them get unfocused, be less serious and
stable so they can cut loose, enjoy themselves and have a
little fun. Also makes it easier to leave the body astrally since
this type usually feels cemented in their body.
RAIN FOREST JASPER: (combination of a blue-green Agate,
Green Jasper & Quartz). Makes one feel expansive and
happy.
LINARITE: Makes one feel very good humored and optimistic
about life.

MOUKAITE: Same as Zebra Agate

REALGAR: (Often mixed with Orpiment). For feeling a sense of balance about one's life and the things in it.

RHODONITE: For feeling and projecting an aura of elegance.

GREEN SAPPHIRE: Good luck stone.

TYROLITE: (Like Chrysocolla). To feel happy and cheerful.

AURA CLEARING & DECORDING: Cording refers to energy that another person focuses on you or in your direction. Freud referred to this as cathexis.

ALEXANDRITE: Inhibits cording. Inhibits others from coming into your space.

FLUORITE: (Fluorspar) Excellent aura cleanser. Hold to forehead for 15 seconds for effect. All colors are equally effective. Colors are blue, clear, purple, yellow and green. Use the color that is most attractive to you for greatest compatibility.

BROWN JASPER: Prevents cording.

WHITE ZIRCON: (CLEAR) Aura cleansing.

TENSION REDUCING:

IDOCRASE: Releases tension. Drains out excess energy. The different varieties of Idocrase affect different types of tension.

CALIFORNITE: (True Green) Releases physical tension.

CYPRINE: (Blue) Releases emotional tension.

XANTHITE: (Yellow) Releases Intellectual tension.

WILUITE: (Yellow, yellow-green, & Brown). Releases instinctual tension.

BROWN or GRAY JADE: (Also called Butterfat Jade). Very relaxing as it drains excess energy from all chakras out through the first chakra. When worn during the day, keeps excess energy from building up and helps one operate from a relaxed state. Temporarily suspends the impact of karmic influences.

RED TIGER EYE: Gives the moving center a break. One can get too hyper or buzzed in a moving centered or physical way. Red tiger eye slows the third chakra down and flushes the excess energy out.

ENERGIZING: (Also see Kinesthetic Center).

BLUE GOLDSTONE: Makes you feel a little peppier if tired--like taking a shower after work. Can relax and feel a little refreshed. Also see Calming.

CAMPBELLITE: Energizes the physical body and stimulates it to move. A good exercise motivator. Also gives the body a greater degree of endurance and stamina.

CRYSTAL, YELLOW: Raising energy; absorbing more energy through the chakras. Makes you feel more energetic. An energizer.

OBSIDIAN, GOLD or SILVER SHEEN: Energizes by getting one in touch with the movement of one's body. Stimulates one to engage in activities that promote bodyily health.

BLACK OPAL: A very energizing stone. Also makes one feel energetically connected to the whole.

SEPTARIAN NODULE: An energizer that keeps the energy moving throughout the body. The concretions are full of Divas which makes you operate more powerfully because you have their energy behind you.

THE HEALER

NEVADA JADE: (Pale green and pink. Also called Nevada Lapis). To become a master healer; really in charge of and in control of your healing powers. Aids in helping and healing others rather than the self.

ZOISITE, GREEN: Enables those in positions of service to really manifest their power and use it appropriately to heal or aid others. Also good for those in service positions of great power such as a director of a research project to find a cure for cancer to manifest very powerfully.

BODY TYPE

Choosing a body type is similar to choosing an overleaf. It is chosen astrally prior to birth and will in some way facilitate the lessons and karmas for that particular life. The effect of body type is less than that of the other overleaves and the effect can be neutralized somewhat by being aware of its workings. Body type will inflluence personality traits and tendencies including physical characteristics, strengths and weaknesses, and psychological tendencies including emotional and intellectual capacities.

There are seven body types which correspond to the Sun, Moon and the five closest planets: Mercury, Venus, Mars, Saturn, and Jupiter. Most fragments will choose a body type that comes under the influence of two or more planets: for example, 70% Venusian, 20% Mercurial and 10% Lunar. Pure body types are rare and are found mainly in mythology, fairy tales or archetypes. There are two additional body types associated with the more distant planets Uranus and Neptune. These influences are chosen more rarely and used for more obscure karmas.

Below are listed the nine body types and the corresponding psychological features of that body type. Below that are listed the Agates that correspond to a particular body type. The use of these Agates allow one to experience the qualities that are associated with that body type. Or, if one has a conflict typical of a particular body type, the relevant stone will help heal it.

BODY TYPES:

SOLAR: Refined features. Slight figure. Radiant. Creative. Lighthearted. Cheerful. Elegant. Dignified. Fun-loving. Child-like. Innocent. Androgynous.

LUNAR: Luminous. Pale skin. Moon faced. Passive. Patient. Tenacious. Sensitive. Imaginative. Maternal. Sympathetic. Receptive. Calm. Methodical. Solitary. Detail oriented. Mathematical. Can have genius intelligence.

VENUSIAN: Full-bodied. Voluptuous. Soft. Warm. Loving. Approachable. Adept in art of harmony. Gentle. Non-judgmental. Sensual. Extremely loyal. Appreciative of Beauty.

MERCURIAL: Slender and quick moving. Intellectually active and perceptive. Clever. Versatile. Able to communicate clearly through speech. Sunny disposition. Youthful appearance.

MARTIAL: Red hair and skin commonly with freckles. Very active physicaly, emotionally and intellectually. Decisive. Freedom-loving. Pioneer. Direct. Brutally honest. Strong leader in crisis. Highly productive. Energetic. Passionate. Highly sexed.

JOVIAL: Santa Claus or Falstaff type. Short and stout. Magnanimous. Compassionate. Generous. Caring and maternal. Philosophical outlook. Breadth of vision. Well-directed mental powers. Good fortune. Sense of justice.

SATURNIAN: Uncle Sam or Abe Lincoln type. Large boned. Prominant features. Serious but gentle appearance. Self-control. Good natural leader. Diplomatic. Moderate. Trustworthy. Paternal. Capacity for long-thought and good memory.

NEPTUNIAN: Dreamy, creative and unworldly in appearance. Large, saucer-like eyes. Idealistic. Spiritual. Imaginative.

80

Sensitive. Subtle. Artistically creative.

URANIAN: Pale or unusual skin. Large bodied. Natural drive towards fame as Yul Brunner or Grace Jones. Independent. Original. Loathing restrictions. Strong-willed. Versatile. Inventive. Sensuous. Humanitarian. Good-willed. Often naturally or deliberately bald.

BODY TYPE AGATES: The following agates correspond to body type.

WHITE or WHITE ON WHITE:	Venusian
BLACK/WHITE Striped:	Mercurial
GREEN/WHITE Striped:	Jovian
GREY or BROWN-GREY/WHITE	Lunar
ORANGE/WHITE (Sardonyx):	Martial
BRIGHT YELLOW:	Solar
ORANGE/BROWN or YELLOW:	Saturnian
BLUE/WHITE:	Neptunian
YELLOW/WHITE:	Uranian
BANDED AGATE:	Plutonian
ARIZONA AGATE⁻	Solar/Venus

RELATIONSHIPS

IN GENERAL: (See also Communication, Sexuality, Reproduction and Higher Kinesthetic Center).

BORNITE: For wider social consciousness, peace, justice, higher principles. Keeps you very aware of your principles. You want to be sure things are fair and are willing to protest if they're not. One is pulled into being concerned with what will work for the society.

CALEDONITE: To feel more friendly and neighborly. Good for those who are wooden in social situations and not very charismatic: will feel more comfortable relating to others.

NEOTICITE: (Purple/red brown). Increases the wearer's ability to seem friendly and outgoing even though inside they may be feeling a little inhibited and closed.

GREEN TOPAZ: Be reserved and benevolent. Useful in situations where another person does something really stupid and you'd rather be benevolent and understanding rather than rub their nose in it and further the karma. Keep yourself from doing something ineffective when someone else already has; i.e., reserved.

STAR SAPPHIRES: Isolation stones. Says: "Don't interfere with me. I want some privacy right now." Color selected

81

depends on frequency at which one vibrates.

    BLACK:1-20 frequency

    BLUE or WHITE: 20-80 frequency

    RED: 80-100 frequency

ZEBRA GNEISS: Anti-prejudice or anti-zenophobic rock. Puts one in alignment with those you regard as different from you. Enables one to feel they can understand other races and other sentient beings such as Whales and Dolphins. Makes it easier to understand how they're thinking and what they're doing.

INTIMATE RELATIONSHIPS: (See also Higher Emotional Center).

LARAMAR: For eternal love. Allows you to keep on loving wherever you've been loving. Very useful when a relationship is undergoing a stress and you feel your love may be jeopardized. Laramar ensures that the love that's underneath all that stuff will still be there.

MANGANOCALCITE: The "adorable" stone. A stone whose effects are noticed by others, but not noticed by the person wearing it. Greatly increases your adorable quotient. Intensifies positive pheromonic potential. Thus, any positive reaction tends to be heightened and any negative reaction a person might have towards you will be toned down.

NATROLITE: Heals foot problems by resolving issues connected with them. People put energy blockages in their feet relating to love issues (right foot) or support issues (left foot). Calms issues relating to love or support depending on color.

    CLEAR or YELLOW: Left foot.

    RED or WHITE: Right foot.

ORPIMENT: For feeling nurtured and emotionally connected with others. Makes you feel you are getting what you want and need from loved ones.

PINK SAPPHIRE: Brings out one's ability to surrender to a cause or another person for the greater good. Can be really devotional and appreciative of the people that you have surrendered to. A very people oriented stone. See goal of submission.

PINK SPINEL: (Pink to red in color). An other-oriented stone: submission and devotion to those you love. Enables one to surrender to and be devoted to another person. Can set one's ego aside when with them and be loving even when its tough. A good wedding ring stone.

STILBITE: (Aqua-blue, pink, peach, white, grey or clear in color). Is very similar to Manganocalcite. Need to have it very near your body for the other person to regard you as adorable. Choose the color you resonate to the best, although all work equally well.

WILLEMITE: Appreciation of people you care about. Similar to Laramar. Continuing to appreciate people you already care about instead of taking them for granted.

ESSENCE TWINS: An essence twin is what is popularly referred to as one's "soul mate."

AMETHYST QUARTZ: (Purple and White stripe). Helps essence twins get along with each other.

BLUE HALITE: Helps to attract an essence twin into one's life. If already acquainted with one's essence twin, this stone helps one to get along with them.

RED SERPENTINE: (Looks somewhat like red aventurine except it's lighter in color and has some brown in it). Helps have good sex with your essence twin. A very pretty rock.

HOME and FAMILY:

CRAZY LACE AGATE: "Intergenerational" stone. Makes children undertand parents and grandparents. Makes parents and grandparents understand children. It encourages the generations to feel they can enjoy one another.

AMETRINE: Good for blending the old with the new, so very helpful for blended families. A blended family is a second marriage with children that are "his, hers, and/or ours."

CAROLLITE: Promotes stability in the home because one feels a desire for rootedness, appreciation for one's home, and enjoyment in focusing attention on it. Don't wear a rock like this, put it on the mantelpiece.

SARD: (A type of quartz). "Homestone". Brings up memories of home and reminds a person of their attachments and family commitments. Those who are without family or home feel more rooted and comforted.

SPESSARTITE: "Homemaker stone." Makes for a happy home life. See chief features.

PURPLE SPINEL: Aids communication with those at least 20 years older or younger than yourself. A generation gap stone.

TURITELLA AGATE: Same in use as Ametrine. See "walk-ins" for fuller description.

SOUL AGES:

SPINEL, BLUE or GRAY: Helps young, mature or old souls who have constant dealings with infant or baby souls to be appropriate in the way they relate.

YELLOW-GREEN TOURMALINE: Helps old, mature, and young souls relate to each other well.

VIVIANITE: Helps one get along with infant and baby souls.

SUCCESS

EMPOWERMENT: (See Power Mode and also Roles for empowering gemsones that relate to a particular role.)

AUGITE: Promotes ambitions. Enables one to pull in what is needed to get ahead and to use one's personal power effectively to realize one's ambitions. Usually found with Green Jade or Serpentine which adds the ability to stay in a tranquil, calm state and not be ripped by one's ambitiousness. Sometimes found with Orange Jade or Serpentine for an ability to be skeptical and not naively trusting.

ANDALUSITE: For empire building. Combines discrimination, power, and perserverance. Similar to Xmas Tree Jasper.

BOOTHITE: For strong charismatic appeal. Inspires others to trust you. Good for those in the public eye.

CACOXANITE: Makes one feel ambitious and, at the same time, very practical about achieving one's ambitions. A powerful stone that enables one to act from a position of authority and power that is very grounded.

CHALCOSIDERITE: Very powerful in its ability to get in touch with and manifest one's ambitions in a positive way.

EUCLASE: Pulls one into a state of striving for excellence and trying to achieve perfection. One wants to be exactly correct on all levels. Good to wear when you want to make an incredibly good impression. Or, if you need to deal with very difficult people in a difficult situation, it will help you remain diplomatic and tactful.

HEMIMORPHITE: (Also called Calamine). Enables you to be assertive, enthusiastic and dynamic in your undertakings.

XMAS TREE JASPER: (Tri-colored: mustard yellow, red-red, and green). An incredibly successful stone. Similar to Andalusite, the "empire builder". A combination of aggressive dynamic energy (red), cool, calculating intellectual energy (green), and uranian energy for a

84

long-lasting impact(yellow). This stone totally empowers you to conquer whatever you've set out to do. Keeps you anchored in mastery and excellence; completely focused and looking ahead to what you're going to accomplish next without getting distracted. Can produce the same effect by combining Garnet, blue Topaz, and Rutilated Quartz. Michael suggests throwing in a little Blue Sapphire for compassion.

OLIVENITE: (Grey/green black crystals). Promotes business by putting you in the mood to do career type work. Makes it easy to focus on work or career issues.

PYROLUSITE: A stone that enhances qualities of determination, willfulness, ambition and conquering. Good for stiffening the spine of a passive, jelly-fish type of person. Young warrior stone often combined with White Calcite. White Calcite is related to the messianic plane and enables you to feel loving and accepting of others. This is the best combination for a young warrior as they might go overboard with this stone and get into clawing their way to the top using other people as a ladder.

MONEY:

ETTRINGITE: Tends to attract money or energy in the form of goods (things that are worth money) into your life.

PYROMORPHITE: Attracts money or energy in the form of goods.

STURMANITE: Attracts money and energy in the form of goods.

ZIRCON, PURPLE: "Penny" stone for monetary resourcefulness. Makes one feel like there will always be money if it is really needed.

ORGANIZATION:

DUMORTIERITE: Encourages a business-like attitude. Use when you want to prioritize, get organized and get things in order. Helps you be more organized, but not necessarily more productive.

GRAPHITE: For organization. Brings in a sense of orderliness; that you like things to be in place and that whatever you're doing, you will do it in an organized fashion.

85

MEMORY

BETAFITE: (Looks like Sandstone). Helps you remember past life lessons.

ENSTATITE: (Brown, grey-green, cat's eyed). Good for short-term memory retention. Useful in taking tests.

RHODOCHROSITE: Increases long-term memory. Also helps remember what was happening while you were wearing it. It can also bring up memories from previous lives.

SKUTTERUDITE: Puts you in touch with past lives. Aids in remembering them. See re-evaluation.

STAUAROLITE: Helps one to remember lessons from the infant cycle.

TUGTUPITE: Sharpens the memory; increases the ability to remember.

KARMA

According to Michael, karma means intensity and can be either positive or negative. Under ideal circumstances we experience karma (intense interaction with oneself or another), process it and complete it. Upon completion of a karma, balance is restored and the experience is neutralized. If we don't complete a karma in one lifetime, then that carries over to another lifetime until we can engage in an interaction with the other person that restores balance. So if you punch me in the nose and then die before I can punch you back, there exists an imbalance in the energy exchange which will have to be completed in another lifetime. It is also important to note that karmic exchanges can be positive.

GRAY CALCITE: Temporarily eliminates karmic influences (neurtralizes the impact). Gives you a break from karmic intensity so you can take a look at the issues in your life from a detached point of view.

HUBNERITE: Brings your karmas in to you. If your life gets boring, use it.

BLUE JADE: Neutralizes the impact of karmic influences. Allows you to see what's going on and remain neutral about it emotionally.

BROWN or GRAY JADE: Same as Blue Jade and Gray Calcite.

LEGRANDITE: For karmic intensification. It brings in karmic

86

lessons through imbalance; it makes you feel unbalanced which propels you into either self karma or karma with another.

PAUA SHELL: Helpful in difficult karmas or soul-level transitions. Reduces stress.

ANIMALS

BERYLLONITE: Balancing and calming to all mammals. Especially useful for calming nervous pets.

BROOKITE: (Grey or purple/black metallic crystals). Increases understanding of the way other mammals think. Good for animal trainers, pet-owners, farmers, etc.

ILVAITE: (Black color) Related more strongly to animals (non-sentients) than humans. Increases the appetite of animals that are off their feed.

POPPY JASPER: Helps you relate to animals. Feel more comfortable with your pets.

MIMETITE: Keeps reptiles balanced.

PHOSGENITE: Helps birds, etc., lay stronger eggs.

STIBICONITE: Balances fish and crustaceans.

THINOLITE: Training animals and communicating with them.

CLEAR TOPAZ: For better relationships with non-human species on this planet; i.e., plants, pets, etc.

VEATCHITE: Reduces fear of animals.

DREAMS

ENARGITE: In general, promotes vivid dreaming, so it can be used by those who want to remember their dreams more.

HERKIMER DIAMOND: For vivid dreaming and astral clarity. Good with rhodocrosite because that will help you remember your dreams. Sometimes includes rutile which is power-chakra energy.

IMAGINATION

BISMUTH: Aids imagination and story-telling abilities.

DRUSY QUARTZ: Same in effect as Quartz, but has a dreamier quality than regular Quartz.

ELINOCLASE: Increases one's ability to use one's imagination.

GYROLITE: Accentuates female energy qualities; unfocus, looking in many directions at once, and creativity.

UVARIVITE: Aids imagination and story-telling abilities.

SPIRITUALITY and TRANSFORMATION

AMETHYST: Balances on all levels: physical, mental, emotional, and spiritual.

CREEDITE: Connects one with the Tao. One feels directly connected with God.

CYANOTRICHITE: Transforming due to its ability to pull you into emotional intensity and depth.

GRANITE: Connects one with the Tao. Opens the seventh chakra. One feels directly connected with God--the supreme reality.

LAVENDER QUARTZ: (Also called Cape Amethyst). Calming. Relieves Stress. Aids meditation and self remembering. Self-remembering is being aware of what one is actually doing and saying on all levels. An intense, supra-self awareness. For this reason Lavender Quartz aids in transformation and self realization.

MALACHITE: Balances on all levels: physical, mental, emotional, and spiritual.

SPHALERITE: (Pisces) (Also called Blende). For transcending ego, for spirituality and empathy. The stone is empathic with you. It senses where you are and empathizes with you. It tries to be in your mood and bring your mood up. This is why it transcends ego -- it takes you beyond the petty problems and into a higher space of calm and who you really are.

BLACK: Warrior
BROWN: King
CLEAR: Scholar
ORANGE/PINK: Sage
PURPLE: Priest
RED: Artisan
YELLOW: Server

CHANGE

ARTONITE: Aids one in adapting oneself to the changes in your life. For example, you got fired and have to look for a new job, or you're moving to Seattle and you don't know anyone there. This stone is 100% female energy and female energy can take on whatever happens; it just engulfs it in its energy pattern because it doesn't have any preconceived ideas as to what is meant to happen the way male energy

88

does. Male energy can lead to disappointment because it has pictures or expectations about what will happen.

COBALTITE: Helps one to integrate one's lessons and pull the various aspects into a coherent whole. Useful for those at the third level of any soul age, for those who are in therapy and for anyone with changes to integrated into their life.

FERBERITE: Allows acceptance of new things, people and places. One is more willing to let go of familiar structures and be more flexible and fluid around changes in one's life.

FRIEDALITE: (Marbled orangy-pink and white). Enables one to feel more at home on the East Coast of the United States. This is also where it is found. Good for immigrants to the U.S. or citizens from other parts of the U.S. who are transplanted to the East Coast.

MILLERITE: This stone starts you eliminating unreasonable prejudice: Beliefs you got in imprinting that have no actual basis in fact. Helps dump them out.

MORGANITE: Heals prejudice and intolerance toward others.

MORRISON RANCH JASPER: Helps you feel more comfortable with important "rituals" in your life that mark a major change or passage to another phase of life. Examples are moving out of the home for the first time, graduating from college, getting married, having a baby, turning 40, etc. Makes you feel capable of handling these changes and seeing clearly what comes up around them.

STICHTITE: (Purple and Pink variety). Aids in completing old cycles and cleaning up one's incompletions. Cycles have a beginning, middle, and an end. Stichtite encourages one to continue through to completion.

ULEXITE: For a philosophical outlook, rising to the challenge, freedom and adventuresomeness. Makes you feel free to do whatever you want to do; that you're not restricted or stuck. Feel that you really can make changes and transform yourself in a positive adventurous way.

WALK-INS

Most of us come into a body around the moment of birth and grow up with the body. A "walk-in" is an essence who comes into an adult body (with the permission of the departing essence) and does not go through childhood.

89

TURITELLA AGATE: Assists walk-ins because this stone is about taking something old and something new and putting them together. This is an Agate that has grown up around tons of little fossils. So, when you're taking an old essence and putting it into a new body, this stone is helpful since it is also a combination of the old and the new. In general, healing to the instinctive center and useful for anyone in this regard.

AMETRINE: (A heat-treated crystal). Promotes a blend of the old and the new and, thus, assists walk-ins in adjusting to the pysical plane. Amethyst is like the high frequency of the Tao, and as it heats in the center it becomes more focused and more physical. Similar to the process walk-ins go through and is probably the best stone for walk-ins.

ROSE QUARTZ, PINK TOURMALINE, & KUNZITE combination: This is an excellent combination for walk-ins: Rose Quartz keeps one in the body; Pink Tourmaline encourages one to go with the flow and not resist and Kunzite is for surrender.

MISCELLANEOUS:

DESAUTEKITE: (Grey/blue rock). Makes you able to predict future trends and assess more accurately the probabilities of various events occurring in the future.

FUCHSITE: Increases appreciation of artistic endeavors. Also enhances one's talent around anything that requires artistic ability, flai or an eye for design.

MARMATITE: (Found with Siderite). Helps neutralize astrological influences. For example, great to wear when Mercury is retrograde or Saturn is transiting your Venus.

PEACOCK COPPER: (Also called Chalcopyrite or Copper Pyrite). A rock that encourages one to be eccentric and to be comfortable, as well, with one's eccentricity. Also raises one's self esteem.

POLYHEDROIDS: Enables one to relate to alien thoughts and cultures

SIEGENITE: Increases eye-hand coordination.

PINK TOPAZ: Integrity and honesty.

BLACK TOURMALINE: Healing for house plants. Has no effect on humans.

WULFENITE: Connects one to the Divas (pre-sentient spirits).

GEMSTONES
An Alphabetical List

ABALONE: Healing, especially for high (50-l00) frequency types. In general, has the same effect as Ivory. Most useful when one has exalted roles, goals or attitudes. Pp. 47,72.

ACCANTITE: Helps one to be more idealistic and optimistic. P.36.

ACHROITE: See Tourmaline.

ACTINOLITE: (Also called Smaragdite). A power stone for Artisans. P. 11.

ADAMITE: A "Specificity" rock. It enables one to focus on the details or specifics of their situation. Produces a quality of particularness. P. 14.

AGATE, ARIZONA: A body type Agate mixing solar and venus body types. Brings out warm, sensuous, sunny, light, and androgynous qualities. P. 81.

AGATE, BODY TYPE: The following Agates correspond to body type. The effect will be to bring out the qualities asociated with each body type. Or, if one has a conflict typical of a particular body type, the relevant stone will help heal it. P. 81.

WHITE or WHITE ON WHITE:	Venusian
BLACK/WHITE Striped:	Mercurial
GREEN/WHITE Striped:	Jovian
GREY or BROWN-GREY/WHITE (Botswana):	Lunar
ORANGE/WHITE (Sardonyx):	Martial
BRIGHT YELLOW:	Solar
ORANGE/BROWN:	Saturnian
BLUE/WHITE:	Neptunian
YELLOWISH BROWN:	Uranian
BANDED AGATE: (with clear stripes).	Plutonian

AGATE, BLUE LACE: (Also lavendar and white in color). Softens stubborness. P. 57.

AGATE, BRAZILIAN: Healing to the kidneys. P. 69.

AGATE, BRECCHIATED: (Also called Tubular or Canal Agate). Erases all chief features. P. 58.

AGATE, CANAL: See Brecchiated Agate.

AGATE, COPCO: Balancing energy combined with loving emotionality. P. 67.

AGATE, CRAZY LACE: "Intergenerational" stone. Makes children understand parents and grandparents and vice versa.

91

It encourages the generations to feel they can enjoy one another. P. 83.

AGATE, DENDRITIC: Balances high-frequency types. P. 66.

AGATE, FIRE: See Fire Opal. P. 32.

AGATE, FLAME: Same in effect as Zebra Agate. P. 77.

AGATE, MOSS and FERN: (Dendritic agate). Healing in general. Balances high-frequency types. Pp. 66, 69.

AGATE, LATTICE: Eliminates headaches. P. 72.

AGATE, LEOPARD SKIN: Very grounding and healing when dealing with heavy emotional issues. Reduces free-floating anxiety. Pp. 47, 75.

AGATE, PLUME: Opens up the expression of sexuality and creativity. Pp. 46.

AGATE, SAGENITE: (Purple with threads of white). Enables one to be more direct and clear in one's expression and communication, particularly artisans and sages. P. 61.

AGATE TUBULAR: See Brecchiated Agate.

AGATE, TURITELLA: Helps one combine the old with the new. Good for walk-ins and blended families. Pp. 83, 89.

AGATE, WONDER: For male sexuality. P. 72.

AGATE, ZEBRA: Helps you enjoy your body. P. 77.

AJOITE: Puts you in a good mood and enables you to be good humored. P. 77.

ALBITE FELDSPAR: (Blue, clear or white in color). Balances, grounds and integrates mature and old priests. Pp. 10, 66.

ALEXANDRITE: Limits and inhibits elements (including people) you don't want from coming into your space. Prevents cording. Pp. 29, 78.

ALMANDINE GARNET: (red with a violet tint). Focused productivity. P. 14.

AMAZONITE: (Blue-green Microcline). Softens self-destruction and greed. It makes you see how unnecessary self-destructive habits are. P. 56.

AMBER: Good for mental clarity. Pp. 7, 44.

AMBER, RED: Calms and eliminates negative emotional influences. P. 44.

AMBLYGONITE: Reduces arrogance by taking the attention off the self. See chief features. P. 55.

  GOLD: For solid types; i.e., a person who's very grounded and organized.

  PINK: For fluid types; i.e., a person who's more flowing, expansive and fluffy.

  CLEAR: Good for all.

AMETHYST: Balances on all levels: mental, emotional, physical and spiritual . Particularly balancing for high-frequency types (50-l00) and for those with extreme male/female energy. Also softens impatience and martyrdom. Pp. 57, 66.

AMETHYST QUARTZ: (Purple and white stripe). Helps essence twins get along with each other. P. 83.

AMETRINE: Similar to Turitella Agate in that it helps one combine the old with the new. Good for walk-ins and creation of blended families. Pp. 83, 90.

AMIANTH: Opens the instinctive center quickly. P. 47.

ANALCITE QUARTZ: A stone with a neutral energy that stabilizes and anchors. P. 75.

ANDALUSITE: For building empires. The Chiastolite variety is the strongest. P. 84.

ANDESINE FELDSPAR: Balances, grounds and integrates mature and old artisans. Pp. 11, 66.

ANDRADITE, DEMANTOID: (Emerald Green) Heals veins. P. 69.
                MELANITE: (Black) Heals skin.
                TOPAZOLITE: (Yellow) Heals synapses.

ANGEL STONE: See Apophylliite.

ANGLESITE: Healing for hardening of the arteries. P. 69.

ANORTHITE FELDSPAR: Balances, grounds and integrates mature and old scholars. P. 66.

ANTIGORITE: See Serpentine.

ANTLERITE: Promotes clear communication and makes it difficult to argue. P. 60.

ANYOLITE: See Zoisite.

APACHE GOLD: Helps one match frequency with someone of a higher or lower frequency than oneself. P. 67.

APACHE TEARS: Assists in communicating with one's essence and spirit guides. Pp. 63, 66.

APATITE: (Colorless, pink, yellow, green blue & violet. Green variety called Asparagus Stone) An acceptance stone that with continued use puts you into higher emotional centers. P. 22.

APOPHYLLITE: (Also called Angel Stone or Fish Eye Stone) Connects one with the cycled-off members of one's entity. P. 64.

APPLE CORAL: See Coral. Pp. 29, 48.

AQUAMARINE: Augments one's power and helps project real strength particularly when you're not sure you are that strong. P. 30.

ARAGONITE: (White, brown yellow & reddish. Also called Tufa). Keeps chakras four, five and six in balance and operating in a blended fashion. Pp. 49, 63.

ARDENNITE: Increases gregariousness and ability to adapt to social situations. P. 60.

ARSENAPYRITE: Helps you match energies (male/female) with someone of different balance than yourself. P. 67.

ARTONITE: Helps one to adapt to and be discriminating about new surroundings. P. 88.

ASBESTOS, LONG-HAIR: Aids in digestion. P. 71.

ATACAMITE: (Green) Enables you to be more discriminating about new surroundings; i.e., a new job, a new house, or a new couch. P. 23.

AUGELITE: A productivity rock for those who are doing artistic, creative projects. Helps with follow through. P. 11.

AUGITE: Promotes ambitiousness. P. 84.

AURICHALCITE: For emotional healing. Pp. 42,75.

AUTINITE: (Brown/green or yellow). Makes you feel more adventurous. P. 77.

AVENTURINE, BLUE: (Also called Blue Quartz or Siderite). Keeps the first chakra open and unblocked. PP. 7, 47, 62.

AVENTURINE, GREEN: Keeps the sixth and seventh chakras open and unblocked. Balances low frequency and extreme male/female types. Pp. 7, 49, 62, 66.

AVENTURINE, RED: (Can also be brown or peach colored). Keeps the second, third, fourth and fifth chakras open and unblocked. Pp. 7, 50, 62.

AXINITE: For infant, baby and young priests. Keeps them from going overboard into total zealousness. P. 10.

AZULISITE: See Labradorite.

AZURITE: (Also called Chessylite). Assists communication generally. Balances low frequency, mid-range male/female energy types (30-700). Softens stubborness. Pp. 57, 60, 66.

BALAS RUBY: See Spinel.

BARITE: (Also called Barytes). Fungus removal. P. 72.

BARTHITE: Helps one be more comfortable with one's sexual idiosyncracies. P. 72.

BASTITE: See Serpentine.

BENITOITE: Healing to the chakras: Pp. 50, 63.
> WHITE: lst chakra
> PINK: 4th chakra
> CLEAR: 5th chakra
> BLUE: 6th chakra
> PURPLE: 7th chakra

BENJAMINITE with AIKINITE: Helps one to be realistic about present and future possibilities. P. 37.

BENJANINITE: Heavy duty instinctive center healer and anesthetic. P. 47.

BERYL, GOLDEN: Heals allergies to plants and pollens. P. 70.
PINK: (Also called Morganite or Bixbite). Heals prejudice and intolerance toward others. P. 89.
COLORLESS: (Also called Goshenite). Balances infant, baby and young scholars. P. 17.
WHITE: Heals dust allergies. P. 70.

BERYLLIUM: (Lilac colored). Connects one with the Messianic Plane. Pp. 43, 64.

BERYLLONITE: (Colorless, white & weak yellow). Balancing and calming to all mammals. P. 87.

BETAFITE: Helps one remember past life lessons. P. 86.

BINGHAMITE: (Goethite plus Quartz). Same in effect as Goethite.

BISMUTH: A "storyteller" stone. Aids imagination and storytelling ability. Pp. 60, 87.

BIWA PEARLS: (Fresh water Pearls). For more eccentric thought. P. 45.

BIXBITE: See Morganite and Pink Beryl.

BLENDE: See Sphalerite.

BLOODSTONE: (Also called Heliotrope). Balances low frequency, extreme male/female energy types. High prosperity conscousness. Pp. 56, 66.

BLUE AVENTURINE: See Aventurine.

BLUE HALITE: See Halite.

BLUE LACE AGATE: See Agate.

BOLIVARITE: Healing for the joints of the body. P. 71.

BONAMITE: See Smithsonite.

BONE: Healing and calming to the instinctive center. Pp. 7, 48.

BOOTHITE: For strong charismatic appeal. P. 84.

BORNITE: For innovation, justice, social-orientation. P. 81.

BOTSWANA AGATE: See Agate.

BOURNONITE: Increases hereditary red-headedness in children of those who wear it. P. 73.

BOWENITE; (Also called New Jade, China Jade or Serpentine. Pale green). Anti-martyrdom stone. Also healing and balancing for female reproductive organs. Pp. 56, 73.

BRACHANTITE: Heals the lungs, esophagus, throat (also cancer in those areas). P. 69.

BRASS: Lowers one's frequency. Mild. P. 67.

BRAZILIAN AGATE: See Agate.

BRAZILIANITE: Balances mature and old scholars. P. 16.

BRECCHIATED AGATE: See Agate.

BRECCHIATED JASPER: See Jasper.

BRONZE: Lowers one's frequency. P. 67.

BRONZITE: (Metallic green-brown). Stimulates one to exercise. Stimulates moving center, in general. P. 45.

BR0OKITE: (Grey or purple/black metallic crystals). Increases understanding of the way other mammals think. P. 87.

BURNITE: Helps one remain realistic and neutral in difficult situations. Pp. 37.

BUTTERFAT JADE: See Jade.

BYTOWNITE FELDSPAR: Balances, grounds, and integrates mature and old kings. Pp. 16, 66.

CACOXANITE: Encourages an ambitiousness that's grounded and powerful. P. 84.

CAIRNGORM: Scottish form of Smoky Quartz.

CALAMINE: See Hemimorphite.

CALCITE, BLACK: For cynicism. P. 36.

    BLUE: Opens and heals chakras. Pp. 50, 62.

    BROWN & GOLD: Connects with the Mental Plane. Pp. 45, 64.

    GREEN: Heals toxic fume damage. P. 70, 71.

    GREY: Temporarily eliminates karmic influences. P. 86.

    RED: (Pink to Salmon). Makes one feel safe to open up emotionally. P. 42.

    WHITE: (Also Iceland Spar) Connects one with the Messianic Plane. Pp. 43, 64.

CALEDONITE: Makes one feel more friendly and comfortable relating to others. P. 81.

CALIFORNITE: See Idocrase.

CAMEO SHELL: Good for eliminating bad habits. Pp. 47, 77.

CAMPBELLITE: Energizes the physical body and stimulates it to move. P. 79.

CAPE AMETHYST: See Lavendar Quartz.

CARNELIAN: Balancing for high frequency, mid-range male/female energy types. Also softens arrogance and self deprecation. Pp. 54, 66.

CARROLITE: Promotes stability in the home. P. 83.

CASSITERITE: A power stone for warriors. P. 14.

CELESTITE: (Also called Celestine). Enables one to adjust to a higher altitude (thinner air) more quickly, particularly if you move from sea level to someplace high. P. 76.

CELENITE ROSE: To keep calcium in your bones. P. 71.

CERUSSITE & BARITE: Fungus removal. P. 72.

CEYLONITE: See Spinel.

CHALCANTHITE: Opens one to higher, emotionally centered

96

experiences. A good channeling stone. P. 63.

CHALCEDONY: (Gray, blue & white). To be more discriminating about what you don't want in your space. P. 23.

CHALCOPYRITE: (Also called Peacock Copper and Copper Pyrite). Raises self-esteem and positive self regard. Also encourages eccentricity. Pp. 54, 90.

CHAROLYTE: A power-mode stone for sages. P. 13.

CHELSET: Helps one be very discriminating about one's appearance. P. 23.

CHERT: See Flint.

CHESSYLITE: See Azurite.

CHIASTOLITE: See Andalusite.

CHINA JADE: See Bowenite.

CHLORITE, GREEN: Attractive to those with female bodies or high female energy. P. 67.

CHLOROMELANITE: (Black Jade and bright green Jadeite mixed together). Very balancing for women in the area of sexual identity. P. 72.

CHROMITE: Softens self-deprecation. Usually found with Kammererite which connects one with the Buddhaic plane. P. 54.

CHRYSOBERYL, GOLDEN : Healing for Australians. P. 69.
   CAT'S EYE: General healing for Asians and South Americans.
   YELLOW-GREEN: General healing for Europeans and North Americans.
   BROWN: General healing for Africans.

CHRYSOCOLLA: Crystallizes feelings of unconditional love, acceptance and tolerance toward others. Pp. 6, 43.

CHRYSOPRASE: (Green Chalcedony) Same in effect as Chrysocolla. P. 43.

CHRYSOTILE: See Serpentine.

CINNABAR: Enables you to be dynamic and a "go getter." P. 31.

CINNAMON STONE: See Hessonite.

CITRINE: Use when you want to slow things down, to create a steady pace or provide a sense of stability. P. 30.

CLAM SHELL: Especially healing for high (50-l00) frequency types. See Shells. Pp. 66, 72.

CLEVELANDITE: Channeling aid. Balances and grounds while channeling. P. 63.

CLINOCHLORE: Helps all roles to get in touch with their server qualities. P. 9.

CLINOZOISITE: (Brown, Light green or gray-green in color). Makes servers better able to serve themselves. P. 9.

COBALT: (An orchid color rock in a brown matrix). Keeps chakras aligned and balanced. A channeling aid. P. 63.

COBALT GLASS: (Blue, Orange and Red in color). Opens the seventh chakra. P. 63.

COBALTITE: Helps one to integrate one's lessons and pull the various aspects together into a coherent whole. Pp. 22, 89.

COLEMANITE: For unfocus and to help one learn to use their female energy. P. 67.

CONACHALCITE: Good when pregnant. Puts mother and fetus in balance with each other. P. 73.

COPCO AGATE: See Agate.

COPPER: Raises one's frequency; makes one feel "buzzy." P. 67.

COPPER, PEACOCK: See Chalcopyrite.

CORAL: (White to red) Wear to create emotional openness and enthusiasm. P. 29.

CORAL, BLACK: Major healer of instinctive centered fear. P. 48.

CORAL, APPLE: Makes one feel deeply warm and caring about others. Takes the fear out of loving. Pp. 29, 48.

CORAL, SPONGE: Recreational sex of the "let's have fun" variety. P. 72.

CORDIERITE: See Iolite.

CORNETITE: Increases fertility. P. 73.

CORNUBITE: A scholar stone. Creates confidence in one's ability to teach. P. 17.

COVELLITE: Puts you in touch with your male energy and helps you use it. P. 67.

CRAZY LACE AGATE: See Agate.

CREEDITE: Connects with the Tao and one's spirituality. P. 88.

CROCOITE: Heals back and headache pain. P. 72.

CRYSTAL; LEADED or NATURAL: (Natural is also called Rock Crystal). Leaded crystal is man made and while it still produces clarity like Rock Crystal does, it does not have the same power or individuality. The differently colored crystals are mostly leaded (man-made) and the different effects are produced by the different colors and not by the crystal itself. The effects are rather mild unless the color occurs naturally in a Rock Crystal. See healing. P. 69.

  BLUE GREEN: Open-hearted acceptance: P. 23.
  BROWN: Opens sixth chakra. Mild effect. P. 45.
  CLEAR: For observation and clarity. Pp. 6, 32, 69.
  GREEN: For sages. Assists communication. Pp. 13, 60.
  LAVENDER TO PURPLE: Balancing physically. P. 69.
  LT. GREEN: Calming. P. 75.
  LT. BLUE: Power mode.

BLUE TINGE: (Occurs naturally). Curbs impatience and martyrdom. P. 57.

GREY TINGE: (Occurs naturally). Discrimination. P. 24.

ORANGE, CHAMPAGNE, TAN: For happiness. P. 77.

PINK: Simplicity in point of view. P. 22.

RASPBERRY PINK: Exuberance, festivity. P. 77.

RED: Dynamism. P. 32.

ROYAL BLUE: Softens martyrdom and impatience. P. 57.

YELLOW: Energizing. P. 79.

CUBIC ZIRCONIA: (All colors) Man-made garnet. Pp. 6, 14.

CUPRITE: Aids in sterility (anti-conception), and abortion. (Don't eat it!). See reproduction. P. 73.

CUPROLITE: For service, practicality and attention to detail. P. 9.

CYANOTRICHITE: Balances hormones and stimulates hair growth. For intensity, depth, and transformation. Pp. 69, 88.

CYPRINE: See Idocrase.

DANBURITE: Curbs Impatience. P. 57

DATOLITE: Produces clearer thinking. P. 44.

DEMANTOID ANDRADITE: Heals veins. P. 69.

DENDRITIC AGATE: See Agate.

DESAUTEKITE: (Grey/blue rock). Makes you able to predict future trends and probabilities. P. 90.

DESCLOIZITE: Removes external aberrant growths. P. 70.

DEUTSCHNER: See Rim Jasper.

DIAMONDS: King Stone. About mastery. Enables one to see ways to handle a situation one desires to master. Certain roles resonate best with certain colors. Pp. 7, 15.

BLACK: Kings

BLUE: Priests

BROWN: Scholars

CLEAR: Warriors

GREEN: Sages

PINK-RED: Artisans

YELLOW: Servers

DIABASE: For fertility and potency. P. 74.

DIASPORE: Observation and clarity. P. 32.

DICHROITE: See Iolite.

DIOPTASE: Healing for the brain. P. 74.

DIOPSIDE: Reduces fever and balances body temperature. Also reduces aches due to temperature imbalance. P. 70.

DOLOMITE: Good for digestion and aids in general bodily health. Kills off aberrant cells and promotes correct bone growth. Very mild in its action. Pp. 70, 71.

DRAVITE: See Tourmaline.

DRUSY QUARTZ: See Quartz.

DUFTITE: Makes it easier to learn any skill that involves the moving center. P. 45.

DUMORTIERITE: Encourages a business-like attitude. P. 85.

EDINGTONITE: Softens grief. P. 75.

EILAT: Keeps one in balance and , thus, able to use higher centers. P. 43.

ELINOCLASE: Increases the ability to use imagination. P. 87.

EMERADA: (Lt. Green Spinel) For fearlessness. P. 76.

EMERALDS: A sage stone and multi-purpose rock. Makes one feel more communicative. Balancing for high frequency, mid-range male/female energy types. Softens arrogance and self-deprecation. Pp. 13, 55, 60, 66.

ENARGITE: A shaman stone. Promotes vivid dreaming. Used by shamans for vision quests. Pp. 64, 87.

ENSTATITE: (Brown, grey-green, cat's eyed). Good for short-term memory. P. 86.

EPIDOTE: (Also called Pistacite). Promotes regular and steady essence growth. P. 21.

ERYTHRITE; Softens martyrdom. P. 57.

ETTRINGITE: Tends to attract money or energy in the form of goods into your life. P. 85.

EUCLASE: Assists one in striving for excellence and making a good impression. Pp. 29, 84.

EUDIALYTE: Related to vitamin absorption, particularly those that are fatty based or occur in complex or yang foods; e.g., nuts, fish, meats. P. 71.

FALCON'S EYE: See Spectrolite.

FANCY JASPER: See Jasper.

FELDSPAR: For integrating, grounding and balancing. Each type is role related. Pp. 9, 10, 11, 13, 16, 17, 66.

ALBITE: (Blue, clear & white. A variety of Peristerite). Mature and old priests.

ANDESINE: Mature and old artisans

ANORTHITE: Mature and old scholars.

BYTOWNITE: Mature and old kings.

LABRADORITE: Mature and old warriors

OLIGOCLASE: Mature and old sages

RED TO BROWN: Mature and old servers

FERBERITE: Allows one to be more accepting of new things, people and places. P. 89.

FERN AGATE: See Agate.

FIRE AGATE: See Opal

FIRE OPAL: See Opal.

100

FISH-EYE STONE: See Apophyllite.

FLINT (CHERT): Heals survival fears. P. 48.

FLUORITE: (Fluorspar) Excellent aura cleanser. Hold to forehead for l5 seconds for effect. All colors are equally effective. Colors are blue, clear, purple, yellow and green and, rarely, red or orange. Use the color that is most attractive to you for greatest compatibility and comfort. Pp. 7, 78.

FRIEDALITE: Enables one to feel more at home on the East Coast of the United States. P. 89.

FUCHSITE: Increases appreciation of artistic endeavors and enhances artistic talent. P. 90.

GALENA: A truth stone. Enables you to know what's true. P. 50.

GARNET: Warrior stone. For productivity and increased havingness. Comes in a variety of colors: rose-red, red and red-brown are colors that relate to warrior qualities. Types are Almandine, Cubic Zirconia, Pyrope and Rhodolite. P. 14.

GEODES (THUNDER EGGS): Observation. P. 32.

GIMELINITE: Increases the delicacy of one's movements and aura of refinement. P. 29.

GIRASOL: See Fire Opal.

GOETHITE: Similar to chlorite, but attractive to those with male bodies and/or high male energy. P. 68.

GOLD: Lowers frequency. Makes one feel more mellow. P. 67.

GOLDSTONE, BLUE: Intellectually calming and refreshing at the same time. Makes you feel a little peppier if tired. Pp. 75, 78.

GORDONITE: Clear muscle-covering healer. P. 70.

GOSHENITE: (Colorless Beryl) Balances infant, baby and young scholars. P. 17.

GOUDIMITE: Decreases arrogance, especially shyness. P. 35.

GRANITE: To connect one with the Tao. Pp. 63, 88.

GRAPHITE: For organization. P. 85.

GREEN AVENTURINE: See Aventurine.

GROSSULAR: Effect varies depending on color.

GRAY to BLACK: Heals the instinctive center. P. 48.

GREEN: (Also called African or Apple Jade. Encourages one to communicate. P. 60.

ORANGE-BROWN: (Also called Hessonite). Balances mature and old sages. P. 14.

LT. GREEN to WHITE: (Also called Hydrogrossular). Healing to the immune system. P. 70.

YELLOW: Calming to sages. P. 13.

GYPSUM: For intellectual clarity, and competency. See centers. Certain colors work for certain roles: P. 44.

CHAMPAGNE: King
CLEAR: Scholar
GREEN: Sage
LT. BROWN: Warrior
WHITE: Artisans
YELLOW: Server
YELLOW-GREEN: Priest

GYROLITE: Accentuates female energy qualities. Pp. 68, 87.

HALITE, BLUE: Helps to attract an essence twin into one's life. P. 7, 83.

HALITE, PINK: For the spiritualist to feel visionary and larger than self. P. 35.

HALOTRICHITE: For fear of heights. P. 76.

HAMBERGITE: Pulls you into a spiritualistic, utopian viewpoint. P. 35.

HAUYNITE: Amplifies shamanic abilities. P. 64.

HAWK'S EYE: See Spectrolite.

HELIODOR: Balances old and mature servers. P. 9.

HELIOTROPE: Same as Bloodstone.

HEMATITE: (Also called Specularite). Useful when you want to re-evaluate or really look something over. P. 22.

HEMIMORPHITE: (Also called Calamine). For assertion, enthusiasm, and dynamism. P. 84.

HERKIMER DIAMOND: (A type of Quartz Crystal). For clarity and observation. Pp. 33, 87.

HESSONITE: (Brown-orange Grossular. Also called "Cinnamon Stone"). Balances mature and old sages. P. 14.

HETEROSITE: To feel more comfortable with emotional openness. P. 42.

HIDDENITE: (Green Spodumene): To connect one with the Messianic or Buddhaic Plane. Pp. 43, 64.

HOLLANDITE: A power stone for warriors. P. 15.

HOPEITE: For healing bone marrow. P. 71.

HORN: Balances the emotional center. P. 42.

HORNSTONE: A name given to several different minerals that are not related to one another except they are all more or less gray. Three we have found are Gray Jasper, Nunkirchner Jasper and Neptunite. Each have different effects on the body.

HOWLITE: Heals the sixth chakra. Pulls one into artistic creation and inspiration. Pp. 12, 45.

HUBNERITE: Brings in karmas. See karma. P. 86.

HUNTITE: Allows one to prioritize so one can productively accomplish everything. P. 15.

HYDROGROSSULAR: See Grossular.

HYPERSTHENE: (Clear black-green or black-brown). Helps reduce fear about being in public view. P. 76.

ICELAND SPAR (CLEAR CALCITE): Connects one with the Messianic Plane. P. 43, 64.

IDOCRASE: Releases tension. The different varieties affect different types of tension. P. 78.
CALIFORNITE: (True green). Releases physical tension.
CYPRINE: (Blue). Releases emotional tension.
XANTHITE: (Yellow). Releases intellectual tension.
WILUITE: (Yellow, yellow-green, & brown). Releases instinctual tension.

ILVAITE: (Black color) Related more strongly to animals (non-sentients) than humans. Increases the appetite of animals off their feed. P. 87.

IMPERIAL JASPER: See Jasper.

INDICOLITE: See Tourmaline.

INDIGOLITE: See Tourmaline.

INESITE: Balances water gain and loss in the body. P. 74.

IOLITE: A very strong dominance and leadership stone. P. 25.
BLUE: (Also called Dichroite or Water Sapphire). Dominance in friendships.
GREY: Dominance in career
PURPLE: (Also called Cordierite). Dominance in sexual and familial relationships.

IRON PYRITE: Helps one match frequency with someone of a higher or lower frequency than oneself. P. 67.

IVORY: Helps to calm basic fears about survival whether issue is real or not. Strong instinctive healer. Pp. 7, 48.

JADE, BLACK: Balances the lower three chakras which involve survival, sex, and power. Integrates these chakras so one is appropriate with all three. Pp. 50, 63.

JADE, BLUE: Neutralizes the impact of karmic influences. P. 86.

JADE, BROWN or GRAY: (Also called BUTTERFAT JADE) . Relaxing. Drains excess energy from chakras. Pp. 7, 48, 78, 86.

JADE, CHINA See Bowenite.

JADE, GREEN: (Also called Nephrite). Produces tranquil attitude. Good when depressed. Pp. 35, 76.

JADE, GREY: See Jade, Brown or Gray.

JADE, LAVENDAR: For Idealism and to produce a more optimistic mood. Pp. 7, 36.

JADE, NEW: See Bowenite.

JADE, ORANGE: Allows one's skepticism to be appropriate. Provides protection for the gullible. P. 36.

JADE, PAKISTAN: Puts you in touch with spiritual energy. Can see the possibilities. P. 35.

JADE, SOUTHERN: (Nephrite that has been heat treated). Puts you in touch with spiritual, visionary energy. P. 35.

JADE, WHITE: Makes it easy to perceive objective reality. P. 37.

JADE, YELLOW: (Soft, creamy color-not really yellow). Promotes understanding of the opposite sex. P. 72.

JAMESONITE: For stability, security, and steadfastness. Good stick-to-itiveness stone. P. 31.

JASPER: All Jaspers and Agates.are very healing. They are the same chemical compound basically and differ in name only.

JASPER, BRECCHIATED: Heals mental stress. Pp. 44, 74.

JASPER, BRICK-RED: Balancing in general. Helps one get along with the same sex. Pp. 66, 72.

JASPER, BROWN: Prevents cording. P. 78.

JASPER, FANCY: "Let's party" stone. (Dark green to violet.) To lighten up those who are extremely male energied. P. 77.

JASPER GREEN: Balances and heals extreme male energy and low frequency types. Pp. 66, 68, 72.

JASPER, GRAY: (Also called Hornstone). Protects and heals the third chakra. P. 46.

JASPER, IMPERIAL: (Purplish/red). For someone who's very unfocused and wants to get focused; for a high female-energied person who wants to get grounded. Conversely, also useful for someone on a very low frequency to feel healed because they're always striving to be higher. Has two different sides to what it does. Pp. 68, 72.

JASPER, MORRISON RANCH: Useful in doing instinctive center work such as past-life regressions. Aids in shamanistic type rituals. Helps one work effectively with changes in one's life. Pp. 48, 64, 89.

JASPER, NUNKIRCHNER: High prosperity consciousness. Same in effect as Bloodstone. Pp. 56, 55.

JASPER, OWYHEE: Useful for solving unusual problems and for pursuing dynamically a difficult problem for a long time. P. 31.

JASPER, PARROT-WING: Very balancing and enables one to use higher emotional and intellectual centers easily. P. 44.

JASPER, PICTURE: For re-evaluation of life issues. P. 22.

JASPER, PINK: Hormone balancing. P. 70.

JASPER, POPPY: For animal allergies. Creates more compatibility with one's pets. Pp. 70, 87.

JASPER, RAIN FOREST: (Combination of blue-green Agate, Green Jasper and Quartz). Makes one feel expansive and happy. P. 77.

JASPER, RED: Aggressive, dynamic energy. P. 32.

JASPER, RIM: Softens all chief features as in Wood Jasper. P. 58.

JASPER, SERAPE: Enhances female sexuality. P. 73.

JASPER, SPIDER WEB: Soothes frayed nerves. Valium like. P. 76.

JASPER, VARIEGATED: Strongest healing stone. P. 70.

JASPER, XMAS TREE: (Tri-colored: mustard yellow, red-red, and green). An incredibly successful stone. Similar to Andalusite, the "empire builder." P. 84.

JASPER, YELLOW: Hormone balancing. P. 70.

JASPER, WILLOW CREEK: Enhances female sexuality. P. 73.

JASPER, WOOD: Softens all chief features: arrogance, self-deprecation, greed, self-destruction, martyrdom, impatience and stubbornness. P. 58.

JET: For cynicism. Wear when it is necessary to go into a situation with all eyes open. Pp. 7, 36.

JOAQUINITE: Healing to the second chakra. P. 46.

KAMMERERITE: Connects one to the Buddhaic Plane and higher kinesthetic experiences. Pp. 46, 64.

KINOITE: Promotes a feeling of peace and harmony. Aids in the easing of grief. P. 75.

KORNERUPINE: (Grass green, pine green,or green brown). Enables one to communicate better and more clearly. P. 60.

KUNZITE: Makes you feel you can accept something that's out of your control and surrender to it. Pp. 26, 90.

KYANITE: Connects one with the Causal Plane. Pp. 45, 64.

LABRADORITE: (Also called Azulisite). Balancing for mature and old warriors. Pp. 15, 66.

LANARKITE: (White-lavendar crystals). Helps you lose weight. Boosts the metabolic rate. P. 74.

LAPIS LAZULI: Emotional Center. Enhances neutral emotional perceptivity. Pp. 7, 42.

LARAMAR: For eternal love. Allows you to keep on loving whomever you've been loving regardless of the stresses in your life or in the relationship. Pp. 43, 82.

LATTICE AGATE: See Agate.

LAVENDER QUARTZ: See Quartz.

LAVULITE, ROYAL: See Sugilite.

LAWSONITE: Calms instinctive fears. Same in effect as Leopard Skin Agate. Pp. 49, 75.

LAZULITE: Same in effect as Lapis Lazuli. Pp. 7, 42.

LEGRANDITE: For karmic intensification. P. 86.

LEPIDOLITE: Connects one with the Buddhaic Plane and enables higher centered experiences. Pp. 46, 64.

LEOPARD-SKIN AGATE: See Agate.

LEUCITE: (Clear or white). Helps clear mucus membranes. Good for colds. P. 70.

LIBETHENITE: Kills off aberrant cells, especially sex cells. P. 74.

LIMESTONE: Extremely healing to the immune system; keeps it in order. Totally cleansing and purifying to the system. Strong grounding rock. Pp. 70, 71.

LIMONITE: Similar in effect to Iron Pyrite. P. 67.

LINARITE: Good humor and happiness. P. 77.

LLANOITE: Promotes unusual thought patterns for the creation of highly unusual solutions to problems or fresh perspectives. P. 12.

LODESTONE: Helps one communicate with dolphins and whales whom are sentient beings. P. 61.

LONG-HAIR ASBESTOS: Aids digestion when worn on the body close to the esophogas or stomach. P. 71.

LUDLAMITE: Exceptionally calming to the instintive center. P. 49.

MAHOGANY OBSIDIAN: See Obsidian.

MALACHITE: Very powerful balancing stone. Balances one on all levels: physical, mental, emotional and spiritual. Balancing for everyone, but especially those in the 50-50 male/female energy range. Pp. 7, 60, 66, 88.

MANGANOCALCITE: The "adorable" stone. Greatly increases your adorable quotient. P. 82.

MARBLE: Balances one's male-energied side regardless of the amount of male energy a particular person has. See balance and frequency. P. 68.

MARCASITE: Similar in effect to Hematite. Helps one re-evaluate life issues. Most jewelry sold as Marcasite is usually Iron Pyrite or Hematite. P. 22.

MARGERITE: (Looks like Rhodocrosite crystals). Allows one to take a look at what's going on in one's life without a sense of struggle about it. P. 22.

MARIPOSITE: "Empire building" stone for artisans and sages. Pp. 12, 14.

MARMATITE: (Found with Siderite). Helps neutralize astrological influences. P. 90.

MELANITE: Heals the skin. P. 69.

MESOLITE: "Go with the flow" rock. Similar to pink tourmaline. P. 27.

METALS: Metals either raise or lower one's frequency. P. 67.

MILLERITE: This stone starts you eliminating unreasonable prejudice: Beliefs you got in imprinting that have no actual basis in fact. Helps dump them out. P. 89.

MIMETITE: Keeps reptiles blanced. P. 87.

MOLYBDENITE: To feel comfortable in the dark. P. 76.

MOONSTONE: Spiritualist. Opens up a person with tunnel vision (only one goal and only one way of achieving it). P. 35.

MORGANITE: (Also called Bixbite or Pink Beryl). Heals prejudice and intolerance toward others. P. 89.

MORION: Dark form of Smoky Quartz.

MORRISONITE: For shamanistic rituals. Helps one get more out of them. P. 65.

MORRISON RANCH JASPER: See Jasper.

MOSS AGATE: See Agate.

MOTHER OF PEARL SHELL: Especially healing for those with ordinal modes, goals, and attitudes. Also strongest instinctive healer. P. 49.

MOUKAITE: For adjusting to and enjoying your body. Same as Zebra Agate. P. 78.

MUSCOVITE: Connects one with the Astral Plane. P. 64.

MYRICHITE: For accuracy and speed of communication. The darker colors are for more intense communication. P. 61.

NATROJAROSITE: Reduces sexual repression and increases passion by lifting the lid off the repression. P. 73.

NATROLITE: Heals foot problems by resolving emotional issues connected to them. P. 82.
  CLEAR, YELLOW: Left foot
  RED, WHITE: Right foot.

NEOTICITE: (PURPLE/RED BROWN). Increases the wearer's ability to seem friendly and outgoing. P. 81.

NEPHRITE: (Mossy, darkish green JADE: may tend toward a brownish color). For stoicism. Makes one more able to be resigned to difficult or unpleasant aspects of your life you cannot avoid. Pp. 35, 76.

NEPTUNITE: (Also called Hornstone). Heals the 3rd chakra. P. 46.

NEVADA JADE: (Pale green and pink in color. Also called Nevada Lapis). To become a master healer. P. 79.

NEW JADE: (Lt. Green: a cross between serpentine and transvaal jade). See Bowenite.

NORTHRUPITE: Increases muscle strength. P. 70.

NUNKIRCHNER JASPER: See Jasper.

OBSIDIAN, BLACK: Same in effect as Leopard Skin Agate. P. 49.

OBSIDIAN, BLACK and BROWN: (Also called Golden Obsidian). Helps eliminate bad habits by reducing craving. P. 76.

OBSIDIAN, SILVER or GOLD SHEEN: Energizes by getting one in touch with the movement of one's body. P. 79.

OBSIDIAN, SNOW FLAKE: (Black and gray). Balancing for high frequency types. P. 66.

OBSIDIAN, MAHOGANY: (Rust-red brown in color). Increases sexuality and sensuality. P. 73.

OKENITE: Balances high female energied types and promotes creativity. P. 68

OLIGOCLASE FELDSPAR: Balances and integrates mature and old sages. Pp. 13, 66.

OLIVENITE: (Grey/green black crystals). Makes it easy to focus on work or career issues. P. 85.

OLIVINE: See Peridot.

ONYX: Balances one's female energied side. P. 68.

OPAL, BLACK: Makes one feel energetically connected to the whole. One resonates to and is very attractive to other people; very likely to be corded. Pp. 46, 79.

OPAL, BOULDER: (Opal still growing in the matrix. Blue with flashes of light). A truly elegant, unusual stone that only people who have a sense of difference would appreciate. Good for working in pentangles to aid the eccentric to come up with wild and crazy ideas. P. 12.

OPAL, FIRE: (Also called Girasol, Sunflower or Sun Opal). Same in effect as Fire Agate. Use when you want to be powerful in circumstances that require action such as teaching an unfamiliar class. P. 32.

OPAL, JELLY: Same in effect as Black Opal, although not as powerful. See higher kinesthetic center. P. 46.

OPAL, SONOMA: Emotionally balancing particularly for mature artisans. P. 12.

OPAL, SUN: See Fire Opal.

OPAL, SUNFLOWER: See Fire Opal.

OPAL, WHITE: Very energizing. Stimulates one to get things done. See kinesthetic center. P. 46.

OPALITE: Pulls excess energy out of the body, particularly the intellectual centers. Relaxing.   Pp. 45, 74.

ORPIMENT: For nurturing and emotional connectedness. P. 82.

ORTHOCLASE: Anti-cancer agent. P. 70.

PADPARADSCHAH: See Orange Sapphire.

PAKISTAN JADE: See Jade.

PARROT WING JASPER: See Jasper.

PAUA SHELL: Helps in difficult karmas or soul-level transitions. See karma. Pp. 75, 87.

PEACOCK COPPER: See Chalcopyrite.

PEARLS: For wisdom. Each pearl is a different inspirational thought or higher truth. Pp. 7, 45.

PEARLS, BIWA: (Fresh water pearls). For wisdom or thoughts that are more eccentric in nature. P. 45.

PERIDOT (OLIVINE): When worn, growth escalates; opens up the adventure box and new challenges abound. P. 21.

PEROVSKITE: Increases cynicism if one is too gullible.   P. 36.

PETALITE: (Clear or pink). Aids in fertility. P. 74.

PETRIFIED WOOD: Calms instinctive fears. Extremely grounding. See instinctive center. P. 49.

PHENACITE: P. 77.
   COLORLESS: Prevents one from forming bad mental habits.
   YELLOW-PINK: Prevents one from forming bad physical habits.

PHOSGENITE: Makes birds, etc., lay stronger eggs. P. 87.

PICTURE JASPER: See Jasper.

PIEMONTITE EPIDOTE: (Cherry red). Very powerful motivator; feel like you're pulsing with "get up and go" energy. P. 30.

PINK HALITE: See Halite.

PIOCHE: Heals the digestive tract. P. 71.

PISTACITE: See Epidote.

PLEONASTE: See Spinel.

PLUME AGATE: See Agate.

POLYHEDROIDS: (A pseudo Agate with a triangular shape). Enables one to relate to alien thoughts and cultures. P. 90.

POPPY JASPER: See Jasper.

PRASE or PRASIOLITE: A power stone for artisans.   P. 12.

PREHNITE: Promotes calm. P. 76.

PROUSTITE: Heals the colon. P. 71.

PSILOMELANE: (Also called Tiger-eye Matrix, Tiger Iron or Quartz Lignite). Power stone for those with the role of king. Pp. 8, 16.

PURPURITE: Keeps the moving center balanced and stamina up. See kinesthetic center. P. 46.

PYRITE: See Iron Pyrite.

PYROLUSITE: A stone that enhances qualities of determination, willfulness, and ambition. P. 85.

PYROMORPHITE: Attracts money or energy in the form of goods. P. 85.

PYROPE: (A type of Garnet. Red with a brown tint). "Abundance" stone: promotes happiness and abundance through productivity. P. 15.

PYROPHYLLITE: Heals and detoxifies the blood. Pp. 70, 71.

PYRRHOTITE: Helps one match frequencies with someone of a higher or lower frequency than oneself. P. 67.

QUARTZ CRYSTAL: (Also called Rock Crystal). For observation and clarity. Pp. 6, 32, 69.

QUARTZ, AMETHYST: (Purple and white stripe). Helps essence twins get along with each other. P. 83.

QUARTZ, ANALCITE: (Forms in squares instead of spears). Very stable energy for cleansing, anchoring and stabilizing. P. 75.

QUARTZ, DRUSY: Same in effect as Quartz Crystal, but has a dreamier quality than regular Quartz. P. 87.

QUARTZ, LAVENDAR: (Often sold as Amethyst or Cape Amethyst). Promotes calm. Relieves stress. Good for meditation. Pp. 76, 88.

QUARTZ LIGNITE: See Psilomelane and Tiger's Eye Matrix.

QUARTZ, ROSE: Assists one in communicating with one's essence and spirit guides. Helps one stay in the body. Pp. 7, 64, 90.

QUARTZ, RUTILLATED: (Quartz with rutile inclusions). Makes one look very powerful; i.e., project an aura of authority, and feel that way as well. P. 30.

QUARTZ, SMOKY: (Also called Cairngorm, Morion and Smoky Topaz). Useful when you want to respond to a person or a situation on a more discriminating basis. P. 24.

QUARTZ, SNOW: An observation stone. Can observe from the place of innocence without so many preconceived notions. P. 33.

QUARTZ, TOURMALINATED. (Quartz with Tourmaline inclusions). Same in effect as Rutillated Quartz. P. 30.

RAIN FOREST JASPER: See Jasper.

RAMSDELLITE: Increases courage. P. 76.

REALGAR: For balanced harmony. Often found mixed with Orpiment. P. 78.

RED AMBER: See Amber .

RED AVENTURINE: See Aventurine.

RED SERPENTINE: See Serpentine.

RED TIGER EYE: See Tiger Eye.

RHODOCHROSITE: Increases memory. P. 86.

GARNET, RHODOLITE: (Rose-red or pale violet type of Pyrope). A warrior stone also for productivity, but related more specifically to one's career. P. 15.

RHODONITE, SOLID PINK or PINK with BLACK: For projecting an aura of elegance. P. 78.

RHODONITE, PINK with BROWN or YELLOW or GREY: . For maintaining one's dignity and "cool" during trying circumstances. P. 76.

RIM JASPER: See Jasper.

ROSASITE: Helps one move out of a negative emotional state expecially when stuck. P. 42.

ROSE QUARTZ: See Quartz.

RUBELLITE: See Pink Tourmaline.

RUBICELLE: See Spinel.

RUBY: Makes one feel giving and happy about being able to be of service to others. Pp. 7, 10.

RUTILLATED QUARTZ: See Quartz.

RYALITE: The generic name for Serape Jasper or Wonder Agate. P. 73.

SAGENITE AGATE: See Agate.

SANIDINE: Anti-cancer agent. P. 70.

SAPPHIRE,DARK BLUE: Enhances creativity. Pp. 7, 12.

SAPPHIRE, LIGHT BLUE: Inspirational. Makes you feel excited about life; that it will really work. Pp. 7, 10.

SAPPHIRE, LILAC: Very balancing for mature and old artisans. Pp. 7, 13.

SAPPHIRE, GREEN: Good luck stone. P. 78.

SAPPHIRE, ORANGE: (Also called Padparadschah) Power stone for scholars. Pp. 7, 17.

SAPPHIRE, PINK: Brings out ability to surrender or to devote onself to a cause or another person for the greater good. Pp. 26, 82.

SAPPHIRE, STAR: See Star Sapphire. P. 81.

SAPPHIRE, YELLOW: Brings in the ability to memorize or retain information: the ability to really learn. Pp. 7, 17.

SAPPHIRE, WHITE: Encourages one to be good to oneself and self-nurturing. P. 10.

SARD: (Variety of Chalcedony). "Homestone." Brings up memories of home and reminds a person of attachments and family commitments. Those who are without family or home feel more rooted and comforted. P. 83.

SARD, LT. BROWN: Aids in digesting vegetable proteins. P. 71.

SARD, RED BROWN: Aids in digesting animal proteins. P. 71.

SARDONYX: See Agate, Body type.

SCAPOLITE: (Also called Wernerite). Balances mature and old kings. Colors correspond to different races: P. 16.

    PINK: Old king; black race.

    WHITE: Mature king; black, red and brown races.

    CLEAR: Old king; red and brown races.

    CAT'S EYE: Old and mature kings; oriental races.

    VIOLET: Old king; white race.

    YELLOW: Mature king; white race.

SCHEELITE: Balances the first chakra. Pp. 49, 63.

SCHORL: See Tourmaline.

SCOLECITE: Balances infant, baby and young artisans. P. 13.

SELENITE: Assists in the digestion and absorption of minerals. Also cleans other minerals. Pp. 7, 71.

SEPTARIAN NODULE: (Combination of Aragonite, Brown Calcite, & Concretions). This combination is energizing and enhances the ability to perceive higher truth and love. Pp. 50, 63, 79.

SERAPE JASPER: See Jasper.

SERPENTINE: Serpentine is the same in its effect as Jade. So, Green Jade has the same effect as the same color in Serpentine, etc.

SERPENTINE, CHARTREUSE: (Pale yellow or chartreuse green in color. Also called Bastite, Antigorite, Chrysotile). Reduces allergic reactions to animals, birds, fish, reptiles, pets and meats to eat. Pp. 70, 72.

SERPENTINE, RED: (Looks somewhat like Red Aventurine except its lighter in color and has some brown in it. The red variety of Stichtite). Helps have good sex with your essence twin. P. 83.

SHATTUCKITE: Puts you in touch with different degrees of your essence. P. 64.

SHELL: Healing to the instinctive center. Similar in effect to Bone and Ivory. See types by name such as Mother of Pearl, Cameo Shell, or Clam Shell.

SIDERITE: See Blue Aventurine.

SIEGENITE: Increases eye-hand coordination. P. 90.

SILVER: Raises one's frequency: more "buzzy." P. 67.

SINHALITE: (Yellow-brown or green-brown). A growth stone. Similar to Peridot. P. 21.

SKUTTERUDITE: Aids in remembering past lives. P. 86.

SMITHSONITE: (Also called Bonamite). Effects vary with

color. P. 50.

GREEN or BLUE: Makes you more emotional especially if blocked. P. 42.

PURPLE: Makes you more psychic. P. 45.

BROWN: Makes you more intellectual. P. 44.

YELLOW: Makes you more moving centered. P. 45.

PINK: Helps make children more psychic. Can also be used by adults, but more useful for children.

SNOW FLAKE OBSIDIAN: See Obsidian.

SNOW QUARTZ: An observation stone. See Quartz.

SODALITE: Balances and increases energy of the second chakra. Increases sexuality and sexual attractiveness. See higher kinesthetic center. P. 47.

SOUTHERN JADE: See Jade.

SPECTRALITE: Stimulates one to exercise. P. 46.

SPECULARITE: See Hematite.

SPESSARTITE: "Homemaker stone." Makes for a happy home life. Also decreases self-deprecation and arrogance. Pp. 54, 55, 83.

SPHALERITE: (Also called Blende or Zinc Blende). For transcending ego, for spirituality and empathy. Effects vary with color. P. 88.

   BLACK: Warrior
   BROWN: King
   CLEAR: Scholar
   ORANGE/PINK: Sage
   PURPLE: Priests
   GREEN: Artisan
   YELLOW: Server

SPHENE: (Also called Titanite). Balancing for those with role of priest. Each color is for a different soul perception. P. 11.

   BLACK & BROWN: Infant priests
   CLEAR: Baby priests
   GREEN and YELLOW: Mature priests
   ROSE-RED: Old priests

SPIDER-WEB JASPER: See Jasper.

SPINEL: Synthetic Spinels have the same effect as naturally occurring Spinels. Effect varies with color.

SPINEL, BLUE or GRAY: Helps young, mature, or old souls who have constant dealings with infant or baby souls to relate to them. Also useful for discrimination. Pp. 24, 84.

SPINEL, DK. GREEN: (Also called Ceylonite and Pleonaste).

Sage stone. Emphasizes wisdom. Pp. 14, 61.

SPINEL, LT. GREEN: (See Emerada). For fearlessness. P. 76.

SPINEL, PEACH: Softens self-deprecation and arrogance. Pp. 54, 55.

SPINEL, PINK/RED: (Also called Balas Ruby). Surrender to those you love. Pp. 26, 82.

SPINEL, PURPLE: Aids communication with those 20 years older or younger than yourself. P. 10, 61, 83.

SPINEL, YELLOW: (Also called Rubicelle). Increases pride. Pulls one into the positive pole of arrogance. Pp. 55, 61.

SPODUMENE, YELLOW or GREEN: (Also called Hiddenite). Connects one to the Messianic and Buddhaic Plane. Pp. 43, 64.

SPODUMENE, LILAC or PINK: (Also called Kunzite). Submission and devotion. Pp. 26, 90.

SPONGE CORAL: See Coral.

STAR GARNET: (Star is formed by Rutile). This combination produces warrior productivity backed by power. P. 15.

STAR SAPPHIRES: Isolation stones. Says: "Don't interfere with me. I want some privacy right now." Color selected depends on frequency at which one vibrates. P. 81.
   BLACK: I-20 frequency
   BLUE or WHITE: 20-80 frequency
   RED: 80-I00 frequency

STAUAROLITE: Helps one to remember lessons from the infant cycle. P. 86.

STELLARITE: Puts you in touch with the highest degree of your essence. P. 64.

STIBICONITE: Balances Fish and Crustaceans. P. 87.

STIBNITE: Bravery and conquering fears. P. 76.

STICHTITE: (Purple and pink variety). Aids in completing old cycles and clearing up one's incompletions. P. 89.

STILBITE: Makes you seem more adorable to others. P. 83.

STURMANITE: Attracts money and energy in the form of goods. P. 85.

SUGILITE: (Also called Royal Lavulite). Very powerful channeling stone. Opens all chakras to higher influences. P. 63.

SULPHUR: Heals plant allergies. P. 71.

SUNSTONE: Effect varies with color. P. 73.
  ORANGE & PINK: For finding sexual relationships.
  CLEAR or YELLOW: For maintaining sexual
  relationships.
  BLUE or GREEN: To get rid of sexual relationships.
SYLVITE: Power stone for servers. P. 10.
TACHIANTITE: Aids the body's cleansing and elimination
  of excesses.   Pp. 71, 74.
TANTALITE: Helps those in repression mode slide to
  passion mode. P. 29.
TANZANITE: Balance high frequency, extreme
  male/female types. See balance. P. 66.
TENNANTITE: Helps one gain weight. P. 74.
TEKTITE: (from Meteors) "UFO Stone." Assists one in
  contacting sentient races from other planets. P. 61.
THINOLITE: Aid in training animals and communicating
  with them. P. 87.
THULITE: See Zoisite.
TIGER EYE: (Yellow-brown). Balancing for low frequency
  types. Also softens stubborness. Pp. 57, 66.
TIGER EYE, RED: Gives the moving center a rest. Allows
  one to stop the action and kick back. Pp. 46, 78.
TIGER-EYE MATRIX: See Psilomelane and Quartz Lignite.
TIGER IRON: See Psilomelane.
TIGILITE: Healing to the instinctive center. P. 49.
TITANITE: See Sphene.
TOPAZ: Effect varies with color.
TOPAZ, BLUE: Puts you more in control; able to lead and
  dominate. P. 25.
TOPAZ, CLEAR: For better relationships with non-human
  species on this planet (pets, reptiles, insects, etc.).
  P. 87.
TOPAZ, GREEN: For benevolence with regard to the
  mistakes of others. P. 81.
TOPAZ, GOLDEN: Pragmatist. Useful for knowing what
  procedures will work in a particular situation. P. 37.
TOPAZ, IMPERIAL: Helps one feel knowledgeable and able
  to exercise all their abilities particularly in scholarly
  pursuits. P. 17.
TOPAZ, PINK: For integrity and honesty. P. 90.
TOPAZ, WHITE: Same in effect as Amber. P. 44.
TOPAZ, SMOKY: See Smoky Quartz.
TOPAZOLITE: See Andradite.
TOURMALINATED QUARTZ: See Quartz.

TOURMALINES: Effect varies with color.

TOURMALINE, BLUE: (Also called Indicolite or Indigolite). Enables you to reject or push the things you don't want away. P. 24.

TOURMALINE, BLUE-GREEN: (Also called Indicolite or Indigolite). Wear to be more open-hearted, giving, and accepting of other people. Invites people in.   P. 23.

TOURMALINE, GREEN to DK. GREEN: (Also called Verdelite). A sage stone. Produces a greater ability to communicate. Pp. 14, 61.

TOURMALINE, PINK to RED: (Also called Rubellite or Uvite). Releases free-flowing energy. Makes you very relaxed. Pp. 27, 90.

TOURMALINE, YELLOW, BROWN or CLEAR: (Yellow variety also called Dravite. Clear variety also called Achroite). Assists in intellectual processing. P. 45.

TOURMALINE, BLACK: (Also called Schorl). Healing for house plants: has no effect on humans. P. 90.

TOURMALINE, WATERMELON: (Bi-color pink and green). For perserverance. Helps one create impression they are stable, reliable and count-on-able. Pp. 31, 68.

TOURMALINE, YELLOW-GREEN: Helps old, mature and young souls relate to each other well. P. 84.

TREE AGATE: See Agate.

TSAVORITE: For self-mastery. P. 16.

TUFA: See Aragonite.

TUGTUPITE: Sharpens the memory and increases the ability to remember. P. 86.

TURITELLA AGATE: See Agate.

TURQUOISE: Centers your being on love and connectedness with others. Pulls one into higher emotional center. P. 44.

TYROLITE: To feel happy and cheerful. Pp. 78.

ULEXITE: (Also called "TV" stone). For a philosophical outlook and ability to rise to the challenge. P. 89.

UNIKITE: For power, dominance and the ability to completely take charge of your own life. P. 16.

UTAHLITE: See variscite.

UVAROVITE: "Storyteller" stone. Aids imagination and storytelling abilities. Pp. 61, 88.

UVITE: See Tourmaline.

VANADANITE: For inspiration. P. 11.

VARIEGATED JASPER: See Jasper.

VARISCITE: (Also called Utahlite). Power and winning.

116

P. 30.

VEATCHITE: Reduces fear of animals. P. 87.

VERDELITE: See Tourmaline.

VESUVIANITE: Being competitive and doing it appropriately. P. 25.

VESZELYITE: Power stone for priests. P. 11.

VICTORIA STONE: Stimulates the emotional center and strong emotions are brought up. P. 42.

VIOLANE: (Violet in color). Balances body temperature and reduces fever. P. 70.

VIVIANITE: Helps one get along with infant and baby souls. P. 84.

VOLCANIC ASH (FUSED): For acceptance and surrender to the inevitable. P. 23.

WATER SAPPHIRE: See Blue Iolite.

WAVELLITE: Healing for bones: Effect varies with color. P. 71.
    BLUE: Small bones.
    BROWN: Teeth.
    COLORLESS: Larger bones.
    GREEN: Medium size bones
    WHITE & YELLOW: Bone marrow.

WILLEMITE: Makes you more appreciative of people you care about. P. 83.

WILLIAMSITE: (Bright green and black). Encourages the appropriate use of discrimination for those who do not have the goal of discrimination. P. 25.

WILLOW CREEK JASPER: See Jasper.

WILUITE: See Idocrase.

WITHERITE: Helps control compulsions. P. 77.

WONDER AGATE: See Agate.

WOOD JASPER: See Jasper.

WOODHOUSITE: Makes you feel you can submit to the greater good. Relates to a goal of submission. P. 26.

WULFENITE: Connects one to the Divas (non-sentient spirits). P. 90.

XANTHITE: See Idocrase.

YOUNGITE: Inspires solutions to problems requiring action on the physical plane. Energizes one to solve difficult problems. P. 15.

ZEBRA AGATE: See Agate.

ZEBRA GNEISS: Anti-prejudice or anti-xenophobic rock. Puts one in alignment with those you regard as different from you. P. 82.

117

ZIRCON, BROWN: Heals headaches. P. 72.

ZIRCON, GREEN: Increases gregariousness. P. 61.

ZIRCON, LT. BLUE: Helps priests or those with priest essence twins feel stable. P. 11.

ZIRCON, PINK: Astral growth. P. 21.

ZIRCON, PURPLE: "Penny" stone for monetary resourcefulness. P. 85.

ZIRCON, RED: Helps ear infections. P. 70.

ZIRCON, WHITE: (clear): Aura cleansing. P. 78.

ZOISITE: GREY: Balances infant, baby and young warriors. P. 15.

ZOISITE, WHITE: Balances infant, baby and young kings. P. 16.

ZOISITE, PINK: (Also called Thulite). Balances infant, baby and young servers. P. 10.

ZOISITE, BROWN: Balances young scholars. Pp. 17, 72.

ZOISITE, GREEN: (With Ruby Crystals, called Anyolite). For servers in positions of great power. Is also empowering for persons of any role who are in a position of service; e.g., healers, or a director of a health project. Pp. 10, 79.

ZOISITE, LAVENDAR: (Also called Tanzanite). Balancing for high frequency, extreme male/female energied types. P. 66.

REFERENCES

1. Van Hulle, JP, Clark, M.C., & Christeaan, Aaron. <u>Michael Study Guide.</u> Michael Educational Foundation: Orinda, 1986.

2. Stevens, Jose, & Warwick-Smith, Simon. <u>A Michael Handbook: Essence and Personality.</u> Warwick Press: Orinda, 1986.

3. Schumann, Walter. <u>Gemstones of the World.</u> Sterling Publishing Company: New York, 1984.

4. <u>The Michael Connection.</u> M.C. Clark, Editor. P. O. Box 1873, Orinda, California 94563.

To obtain additional copies of this book, please write or call:

MICHAEL EDUCATIONAL FOUNDATION
10 Muth Drive, Orinda, Ca 94563
415-254-4730

<u>The Michael Educational Foundation</u> provides open Michael study groups and private channeling sessions to all who are interested.